THE WORLD OF TIBETAN BUDDHISM

An Overview of Its Philosophy and Practice

The WORLD of TIBETAN BUDDHISM

An Overview of Its Philosophy and Practice

TENZIN GYATSO
the Fourteenth Dalai Lama

Translated, edited, and annotated by
GESHE THUPTEN JINPA

Foreword by Richard Gere

WISDOM PUBLICATIONS • BOSTON

First printing, 1995

WISDOM PUBLICATIONS
361 Newbury Street
Boston, Massachusetts 02115

© Tenzin Gyatso, the Fourteenth Dalai Lama 1995
© Geshe Thupten Jinpa, English translation 1995
All rights reserved.

Library of Congress Cataloging-in-Publication Data

Bstan-'dzin-rgya-mtsho, Dalai Lama XIV, 1935–
    The world of Tibetan Buddhism : an overview of its philosophy
and practice / Tenzin Gyatso, the Fourteenth Dalai Lama ; translated,
edited, and annotated by Geshe Thupten Jinpa.
        p.   cm.
    Includes bibliographical references and index.
    ISBN 0-86171-097-5 (pbk : alk. paper) :
    1. Buddhism—China—Tibet. 2. Buddhism—Doctrines. I. Thupten
Jinpa. II. Title.
BQ7610.B77   1994
294.3'923—dc20   94-30512

00 99 98 97 96

6 5 4 3 2

Cover photograph © Clive Arrowsmith 1994
Courtesy of the Office of Tibet, London

Designed by: L·J·SAWLit⸱

Set in Adobe Garamond Font Family, Diacritical Garamond and Bullfinch.

Wisdom Publications' books are printed on acid-free paper and meet the guidelines for permanence and durability of the Committee on Production Guidelines for Book Longevity of the Council on Library Resources.

Printed in the USA

CONTENTS

FOREWORD

THE GERE FOUNDATION is honored to continue its sponsorship of important books by His Holiness the Dalai Lama published by Wisdom Publications, the first two in the series being *Opening the Eye of New Awareness* and *The Meaning of Life from a Buddhist Perspective*.

In the present volume, *The World of Tibetan Buddhism*, beautifully translated and edited by Geshe Thupten Jinpa, His Holiness offers a clear and penetrating overview of Tibetan Buddhist practice from the Four Noble Truths to Highest Yoga Tantra with, as always, special emphasis on the practices of love, kindness, and universal responsibility. He asks us to be mindful and present in the moment, to be constantly vigilant in monitoring our attitudes, actions, and motivations, and to engage in a thorough-going research on our own mental functioning and examine the possibility of making some positive changes within ourselves. Not easy tasks! Few of us are capable of the monumental courage and iron determination required to achieve the enlightened state of Śākyamuni, Nāgārjuna, Milarepa, or Tsongkhapa, or the other saints and heroes. But we can, with sustained practice, bring more clarity to our minds and feel the warmth of our opening hearts.

Recipient of the 1989 Nobel Prize for Peace, the Dalai Lama is universally respected as one of our greatest spiritual friends. He is the product of an unbroken lineage extending back 2,500 years to the historical Buddha. His forty-five years as a spiritual teacher and political leader are unique in our time. He has often said, "My religion is kindness."

Since the Chinese invasion of independent Tibet in 1950 and his harrowing escape to India in 1959, His Holiness has worked tirelessly to free his people from a systematic genocide that has killed 1.2 million Tibetans—one fifth of the pre-invasion population. His Holiness's unfaltering compassion for even those who continue to destroy his country is the mark of a true and reliable bodhisattva. This book is a wondrous opportunity for us all to make contact with such a man and his teachings.

The Gere Foundation is proud to be associated with His Holiness and his message of universal responsibility and peace, and pleased to support Wisdom Publications in its efforts to promote these ideals. May this book help bring happiness and the causes of future happiness to all beings.

Richard Gere
New York

PREFACE

OVER A PERIOD of four days in the spring of 1988, His Holiness the Dalai Lama gave a series of lectures on Tibetan Buddhism in London organized by the Tibet Foundation, London. His lectures were, as usual, conducted in a personal and informal style that, nevertheless, in no way compromised the seriousness and the profundity of the subject matter. Looking back, I feel that those lectures marked an important turning point in His Holiness's method of teaching Buddhism to a modern audience. On that occasion, he put into full swing a novel but sophisticated system of presenting the Buddhist path. Based on four simple premises, that there is suffering, that it has an origin, that there is an end to suffering, and finally, that there is a method for ending suffering, His Holiness presents the entire superstructure of Tibetan Buddhism—its philosophy and practice—including the esoteric path of Vajrayana Buddhism. He beautifully demonstrates how all aspects of the Tibetan Buddhist path must and can be perceived as both emerging from and being firmly rooted in the framework of the Four Noble Truths. In short, His Holiness shows us with convincing explanation how Tibetan Buddhism is, in the true sense of the phrase, "complete Buddhism." The result is a unique overview of Tibetan Buddhism that combines His Holiness's incisive, penetrating insight, profound reflective analysis, and deep spiritual experience, woven with a breathtaking scope of scholarship in all areas of Buddhist thought—all of this, of course, in a style that never fails to radiate a joyful exuberance of life and true affection toward all.

It has been a real joy to work on this project, and I am very happy that now others can also share in the experience. Many people have made significant contributions towards the success of this endeavor. I would like to thank Sally Ward for undertaking the difficult task of transcribing the tapes from the teachings, and Venerable Sarah Thresher, my first editor at Wisdom, for doing a second transcription with the necessary initial editing. I would also like to thank my editor at Wisdom, Venerable Connie Miller, for her valuable comments and criticisms, which contributed a great deal toward improving the English. My thanks also go to Vincent and especially Maria Montenegro and Robert Chilton for hours and hours of editing and research.

It has taken a long time for the lectures to appear in book form. As much as I had wished to see this teaching published, three years of study at Cambridge, England, between 1989 and 1992 delayed work on the manuscript. In retrospect, however, this delay has had a significant consequences in that when I finally had the time to work on the book, I was in a better position to appreciate the subtleties of many important English philosophical terms. For this, I am deeply grateful to the Inlaks Foundation, London, and my friends Geoff Jukes, Morna White, and Isabelle White, whose generosity made it possible for me to study at Cambridge.

In this book, I have attempted to adopt a style of translation that reflects, as faithfully as possible, His Holiness's thoughts as if he were expressing them in English. In this, I have had a ready guideline in His Holiness's own lectures as many of them have been at least partially given in English. These lectures often present a comprehensive overview of Tibetan Buddhism; correspondingly, I have tried to provide extensive footnotes and a bibliography for the benefit of those who wish to explore specific areas of Tibetan Buddhism in greater depth. For similar reasons, a glossary of important terms with their Tibetan and Sanskrit equivalents has been compiled. For their assistance in providing Tibetan and Sanskrit transliteration equivalents, as well as checking the translation of textual citations, I would like to thank John Dunne, Sarah McClintock, David Reigle, Venerable Michael Roach, and Artemus Engle. I would also like to thank Sophie Boyer for reading the entire manuscript and providing a valuable lay perspective.

It is my sincere hope that this book will bring joy into the hearts of many people and a deeper appreciation of the richness of the Tibetan spiritual tradition.

Geshe Thupten Jinpa
Gaden, India

TECHNICAL NOTE

TIBETAN NAMES and terms that appear in the body of the text have been rendered phonetically. In the bibliography, the glossary, and in parenthetical references, Tibetan names and titles are romanized according to the system devised by Turrell Wylie ("A Standard System of Tibetan Transcription," Harvard Journal of Asiatic Studies, Vol. 22, 1959, pp. 261–7), with the exception that the inital root letter of a name or title is capitalized. Sanskrit transliterations follow the standard, internationally recognized system. I have deliberately minimized the use of Tibetan and Sanskrit words within the main body of the text so as not to impede the flow of the presentation. The glossary lists the Tibetan (and occasionally the Sanskrit) terms that correspond to the English translation equivalents used herein. Titles of texts are italicized: sutras, tantras, and Tibetan commentarial materials are referred to by the English translation of their titles; Indian treatises are referred to by their Sanskrit title. All translations from scriptural sources are my own except where noted otherwise.

THE WORLD OF TIBETAN BUDDHISM

An Overview of Its Philosophy and Practice

INTRODUCTION

BROTHERS AND SISTERS, I am very happy to be here and to meet people who are taking a keen interest in the Buddhadharma. I can see many familiar faces in the audience and am very glad to have this opportunity to spend some time with you once more.

During the next three days, I will be speaking on Buddhist thought and practice according to the Tibetan tradition. My talks here will follow two main themes. As to the first [Parts 1 and 3], I will be giving a general introduction to the Buddhist path, a broad outline of the theories and practices of Tibetan Buddhism. I usually explain that the Buddhism of Tibet is perhaps the most complete form of Buddhism. It includes all the essential teachings of the various traditions of Buddhism that exist in different parts of the world today. Since many of you have received a number of tantric initiations and teachings, I think an overview of Tibetan Buddhism for the purpose of providing a comprehensive framework of the Buddhist path may prove helpful in deepening your understanding and practice of Dharma.

The second theme [Part 2] concerns the altruistic attitude that characterizes a bodhisattva. In drawing from Śāntideva's *Bodhicaryāvatāra* (*Guide to the Bodhisattva's Way of Life*), I will offer some comments on important sections of the text, concentrating mainly on the practices of love, kindness, and compassion. Intimately related to these practices are the issues of how to cultivate tolerance as well as the appropriate attitudes one should adopt towards one's enemy.

During these first three days, instead of being the Dalai Lama or Bhikṣu Tenzin Gyatso, I am Professor Tenzin Gyatso. On the fourth day, however, there will be a Green Tārā initiation, and on that day I will become Guru Bhikṣu Tenzin Gyatso!

As I mentioned earlier, a number of us here already know each other. Since our last meeting, many of us have led very busy lives. Whether we are doing something good and worthwhile with our lives or not, time never waits but keeps flowing. Not only does time flow unhindered, but correspondingly our life too keeps moving onward all the time. If something has gone wrong, we cannot turn back time and try again. In that sense, there is no genuine second chance. Hence, it is crucial for a spiritual practitioner constantly to examine his or her attitudes and actions. If we examine ourselves every day with mindfulness and mental alertness, checking our thoughts, motivations, and their manifestations in external behavior, a possibility for change and self-improvement can open within us. Although I myself cannot claim with confidence to have made any remarkable progress over the years, my desire and determination to change and improve is always firm. From early morning until I go to bed and in all situations of life, I always try to check my motivation and be mindful and present in the moment. Personally, I find this to be very helpful in my own life.

Over the three days we spend together, I shall be discussing various methods that we can employ as tools to examine ourselves, enabling us to embark upon a path of self-discovery and development. Taking your own body and mind as the laboratory, see if you can use these different techniques: that is to say, engage in some thorough-going research on your own mental functioning, and examine the possibility of making some positive changes within yourself. This is how a practicing Buddhist should perceive all the essential elements of the Buddha's teaching. There are also people here who, although not considering themselves practicing Buddhists, have a genuine desire to learn more about Buddhism in general, and the Buddhism of Tibet in particular.

This also includes those who, while practicing their own religion, take a keen interest in other spiritual traditions. I am certain that they can find within the Buddhist teachings various common concerns, such as meditation or contemplation on love and compassion, that can be incorporated into their own tradition and practice. Hence, such an ecumenical pursuit has great potential for benefit. Finally, there might be some people here who do not have any particularly strong feeling for spirituality but have come with honest curiosity and openness. These people can just sit and listen to my talks as one listens to a lecture. If, in the course of listening, you find something interesting, you can pay closer attention. Similarly, if there is nothing of much interest and value, you can take the session as a time for rest. However, if you do use it as rest time, please do so discreetly. Especially if you happen to doze off, do not start snoring, for you might disturb your neighbors!

PART I

GENERAL BUDDHISM

1

THE DIVISIONS OF THE VEHICLES

VARIOUS SYSTEMS OF THOUGHT and practice are mentioned in classical Buddhist literature.[1] Such systems are referred to as *yānas* or "vehicles." There are, for instance, the various vehicles of humans and divine beings in addition to the Buddhist vehicles: the vehicle of individual liberation (*hīnayāna*), the vehicle of universal salvation (*mahāyāna*), and the vehicle of tantra (*vajrayāna*). In this context, vehicles of humans and divine beings refer to systems that outline the essential training and methods for both fulfilling the major aspirations of this life and, in addition, obtaining a favorable rebirth as either a human or a divine being. Such systems emphasize the importance of maintaining an ethically sound lifestyle—grounded in refraining from engaging in negative actions—since leading a life of righteousness and good behavior is perceived to be the most crucial factor for ensuring a favorable rebirth.

The Buddha also spoke of another category of vehicle, the Brahma Vehicle, comprising principally those techniques of meditation that aim at achieving the highest possible form of life within *samsara*, the karmically conditioned cycle of existence. Such meditative techniques include, among other things, withdrawing the mind from all external objects, which leads to a state of single-pointedness. The meditative states experienced as a result of having generated single-pointedness of mind are altered states of consciousness that, in terms of their phenomenological aspects and also their mode of engagement with objects, closely correspond to states of existence in the form and formless realms.[2]

From a Buddhist point of view, all these diverse systems are worthy of respect since they all have the potential to bring about great benefit to a large number of sentient beings. However, this does not mean that all these systems are complete in themselves in presenting a path leading to full liberation from suffering and from the cycle of existence. Genuine freedom and liberation can only be achieved when our fundamental ignorance, our habitual misapprehension of the nature of reality, is totally overcome. This ignorance, which underlies all our emotional and cognitive states, is the root factor that binds us to the perpetual cycle of life and death in samsara. The system of thought and practice that presents a complete path towards liberation from this bondage is called the vehicle of the Buddha (*buddhayāna*).

Within the Buddha's Vehicle there are two major systems of thought and practice: the Individual Vehicle, or Hinayana, and the Universal Vehicle, or Mahayana. The former includes the Theravāda system, which is the predominant form of Buddhism in many Asian countries, such as Sri Lanka, Thailand, Burma, Cambodia, and others. In classical Buddhist literature, the Individual Vehicle is described as having two main divisions: the Hearers' Vehicle and the Solitary Realizers' Vehicle. A principal difference between the Individual Vehicle and the Universal Vehicle exists in their views on the Buddhist doctrine of selflessness and the scope of its application. The Individual Vehicle expounds the view of selflessness only in relation to person or personal identity but not in relation to things and events in general, whereas in the Universal Vehicle, the principle of selflessness is not confined to the limited scope of the person but encompasses the entire spectrum of existence, all phenomena. In other words, the Universal Vehicle system understands selflessness as a universal principle. Interpreted in this way, the principle of selflessness acquires greater profundity. According to the Universal Vehicle teachings, it is only when a practitioner's experience of selflessness is rooted in this universal interpretation that the experience will bring about the elimination of the delusions and their underlying states of ignorance. It is by eliminating these underlying states of ignorance that we are able to cut off the root of samsara. Furthermore, a profound experience of selflessness can also lead, ultimately, to full enlightenment, a state of total freedom from the subtle imprints and the obstructive habitual tendencies created by our misconception of the nature of reality. The system of thought and practice which presents such a view of selflessness is called Mahayana, the Universal Vehicle.

The Tantric Vehicle, or Vajrayana, which is considered by the Tibetan tradition to be the highest vehicle, is included within the Universal Vehicle. In addition to meditative practices for enhancing one's realization of emptiness and *bodhicitta*,[3] this system also includes certain advanced techniques for utilizing the various elements of the physical body in one's meditative practice. Such feats are accomplished on the basis of sophisticated yogic practices that principally involve mentally penetrating the essential points within the body where the *cakras*, or energy centers, are located. By means of this subtle and refined coordination of mind and body, the practitioner is able to accelerate the process of getting at the root of ignorance and completely overcoming its effects and imprints, a process that culminates, finally, in the realization of full enlightenment. This feature—of engaging in meditative practices involving the subtle coordination of both mental and physiological elements within the practitioner—is unique to the Tantric Vehicle.

I shall now briefly explain the historical background of Buddhism as we now know it. According to the Kashmiri pandit Śākya Śrī, who came to Tibet in the early thirteenth century, the Buddha was born in India about 2,500 years ago. This accords with the standard position of the Theravāda tradition, but according to some Tibetan scholars, the Buddha appeared in the world more than 3,000 years ago.[4] There is also a third opinion that dates the Buddha's birth to sometime in the eighth century B.C.E. When reflecting on these conflicting opinions regarding what is perhaps the most crucial date in Buddhist history, sometimes I feel that it is quite embarrassing that still no consensus exists on the key question of when the teacher Śākyamuni Buddha actually lived! I seriously think that it would be helpful if, with due respect, scientific tests were carried out on the various relics that are believed to be genuine relics of the Buddha. These relics can be found in countries like India, Nepal, and Tibet. Perhaps scientific experiments on those relics using sophisticated modern technology and chemicals could establish with greater accuracy the dates of the Buddha's existence. This would be very helpful. In the past, erudite Buddhists tried to prove their own version of the historical facts surrounding the Buddha's life mainly through logic and argumentation. Given the nature of the question, however, I think such types of proof can never be conclusive.

Despite conflicting assertions regarding the historical reckoning of his birth, there is a general consensus in the literature as to the key events of the Buddha's life. We know that the Buddha was originally an ordinary person like ourselves, with all the basic faults and weaknesses of a human being. He was born into a royal family, married, and had a son. Later, however, he came into contact with the unsatisfactory suffering nature of life in the form of unexpected encounters with people afflicted by sickness, old age, and death. Deeply disturbed by these sights, the prince eventually left the palace and renounced his comfortable and sheltered princely way of life. His initial reaction to these experiences was to adopt the austere lifestyle of an ascetic, engaging in a spiritual path involving great physical penances. Later, he discovered that the true path out of suffering lies in a middle way between the extremes of strict asceticism and self-indulgent luxury. His single-minded spiritual pursuit ultimately resulted in his full awakening, or enlightenment: buddhahood.

I feel that the story of the Buddha's life holds great significance for us. It exemplifies the tremendous potentials and capacities that are intrinsic to human existence. For me, the events that led to his full enlightenment set an appropriate and inspiring example for his followers. In short, his life makes the following statement: "This is the way that you should pursue your spiritual path. You must bear in mind that the attainment of enlightenment is not an easy task. It requires time, will, and perseverance." Therefore, right from the beginning, it is crucial to harbor no illusions of a swift and easy path. As a spiritual trainee, you must be prepared to endure the hardships involved in a genuine spiritual pursuit and be determined to sustain your effort and will. You must anticipate the multiple obstacles that you are bound to encounter along the path and understand that the key to a successful practice is never to lose your determination. Such a resolute approach is very important. The story of the Buddha's personal life, as we have seen, is the story of someone who attained full enlightenment through hard work and unwavering dedication. It is ironic that sometimes we seem to believe that we, who are following in the footsteps of the Buddha, can somehow realize full enlightenment with greater ease and less effort.

2

THE FIRST TURNING
OF THE WHEEL OF DHARMA

THE FOUR NOBLE TRUTHS

ACCORDING TO POPULAR LEGEND, following his full enlighten-ment the Buddha remained silent and did not give any teachings for forty-nine days. The first public teaching he gave was to the five ascetics who had been his colleagues when he was leading the life of a mendicant. Having realized that asceticism does not lead to freedom from suffering, the Buddha—then called Siddhārtha Gautama—had given up his penances and parted company with his fellows. His five colleagues had resented what they saw as a betrayal and vowed never to associate with him. For them, this change in Siddhārtha had indicated a failure to sustain his commitment to the life of asceticism. However, when they met him after his enlightenment, they felt sponta-neously drawn toward him. It was to these five former colleagues that the Buddha gave his first public teaching at Deer Park in Sarnath.[5]

In this discourse, which became known as the first turning of the wheel of Dharma,[6] the Buddha taught the principles of the Four Noble Truths. As most of you might know, these Four Truths are the truth of suffering, the truth of the origin of suffer-ing, the truth of the cessation of suffering, and the truth of the path leading to this cessation.

According to the sutra concerning the first turning, when the Buddha taught the Four Noble Truths, he taught them within the context of three factors: the nature of the truths themselves, their specific functions, and their effects, or complete attainment. The first factor describes the nature of the individual truths. The second explains the importance of comprehending the specific significance of each for the practitioner: namely, suffering must be recognized, and its origin, eliminated; and the cessation of suffering must be actualized, and the path to cessation, realized. In the context of the third factor, the Buddha explained the ultimate result, or complete attainment, of the Four Noble Truths—that is, the completed recognition of suffering, the completed abandonment of the origin of suffering, the completed realization of the cessation of suffering, and the completed actualization of the path to cessation. I personally find the teaching on the Four Noble Truths to be very profound. This teaching lays down the blueprint for the entire body of Buddhist thought and practice, thus setting up the basic framework of an individual's path to enlightenment. I shall elaborate on this further.

What we desire and seek is to have happiness and overcome suffering. This yearning to have happiness and avoid pain and suffering is innate to all of us and needs no justification for its existence or validity. However, happiness and suffering do not arise from nowhere. They arise as consequences of causes and conditions. In brief, the doctrine of the Four Noble Truths states the principle of causality. Keeping this crucial point in mind, I sometimes remark that all of Buddhist thought and practice can be condensed into the following two principles: (1) adopting a world view that perceives the interdependent nature of phenomena, that is, the dependently originated nature of all things and events, and (2) based on that, leading a non-violent and non-harming way of life.

Buddhism advocates the conduct of non-violence on the basis of two simple and obvious premises: (1) as sentient beings, none of us wants suffering, and (2) suffering originates from its causes and conditions. The Buddhist teachings further assert that the root cause of our pain and suffering lies in our own ignorant and undisciplined state of mind. Therefore, if we do not desire suffering, the logical step to take is to refrain from destructive actions, which naturally lead to consequent experiences of pain and suffering. Pain and suffering do not exist in isolation; they come about as the results of causes and conditions. It is in understanding the nature of suffering and its relation to causes and conditions that the principle of dependent origination plays a crucial role. In essence, the principle of dependent origination states that an effect is dependent upon its cause. So, if you don't want the result, you should strive to put an end to its cause.

Within the Four Truths, we find two distinct sets of cause and result operating: suffering is the result, and the origin of suffering is its cause; in like manner, the true cessation of suffering is peace, the result, and the path leading to it is the cause of that peace.

The happiness we seek, a genuine lasting peace and happiness, can be attained only through the purification of our minds. This is possible if we cut the root cause of all suffering and misery— our fundamental ignorance. This freedom from suffering, the true cessation, can come about only when we have successfully seen through the illusion created by our habitual tendency to grasp at the intrinsic existence of phenomena and, thereby, gained insight that penetrates into the ultimate nature of reality. To attain this, however, the individual must perfect the three higher trainings.[7] The training in insight, or wisdom, acts as the actual antidote to ignorance and its derivative delusions. However, it is only when training in higher insight is conjoined with a highly developed faculty of single-pointedness of the mind that all of one's energy and mental attention can be focused on a chosen object of meditation without distraction. Hence, the training in higher concentration is an indispensable factor in advanced stages of application of the wisdom gained through insight. However, in order for both the trainings in higher concentration and higher insight to be successful, the practitioner must first establish a stable foundation of morality by adopting an ethically sound way of life.

THE THREE HIGHER TRAININGS

Just as there are three types of higher trainings: in ethics, concentration, and wisdom, the Buddhist scriptures fall into three main divisions: discipline, sets of discourses, and metaphysical knowledge. When one is able to undertake a genuine practice of these three trainings, based on the study of the three scriptural collections, and to impart the same to others, it can truly be said that one is upholding the Buddhadharma. The need to engage in these three higher trainings is equal for both men and women. In terms of the importance of study and practice, no distinctions can be made among practitioners on the basis of gender. However, there are certain differences in the monastic rules of ethical training depending on the gender of the practitioner.

The basic foundation of the practice of morality is to refrain from ten unwholesome actions: three pertaining to the body, four pertaining to speech, and three pertaining to thought.

The three physical non-virtues are: (1) killing: intentionally taking the life of a living being, whether a human being, an animal, or even an insect; (2) stealing: taking possession of another's property without his or her consent, regardless of its value; and (3) sexual misconduct: committing adultery. The four verbal non-virtues are: (4) lying: deceiving others through spoken word or gesture; (5) divisiveness: creating dissension by causing those in agreement to disagree or those in disagreement to disagree further; (6) harsh speech: verbally abusing others; and (7) senseless speech: talking about foolish things motivated by desire and so forth. The three mental non-virtues are: (8) covetousness: desiring to possess something that belongs to someone else; (9) harmful intent: wishing to injure others, whether in a great or small way; and (10) wrong view: holding that such things as rebirth, the law of cause and effect, or the Three Jewels[8] do not exist. The morality practiced by a spiritual trainee in the context of explicitly adopting a certain ethical way of life in the form of precepts is known as the discipline of individual liberation, or *prātimokṣa*.

In terms of the nature and specific enumeration of the precepts, four major traditions emerged in ancient India and later branched into eighteen sub-schools.[9] Each of the four main branches had its own version of the *Individual Liberation Sutra* (*Prātimokṣasūtra*)—the traditional record of the Buddha's disciplinary advice that enumerates the ethical precepts and lays down the basic guidelines for a monastic life. The system of monasticism and its underlying ethical rules practiced in the Tibetan tradition is that of Mūlasarvāstivādin school. According to the *Individual Liberation Sutra* of this school, which is in Sanskrit, there are 253 precepts for a fully ordained monk and 364 for a fully ordained nun. This differs from the Theravāda tradition in which the Pali version of the *Individual Liberation Sutra* lists 227 precepts for a monk and 311 for a nun.

The practice of morality—guarding your three doors of body, speech, and mind from indulging in unwholesome activities—equips you with mindfulness and conscientiousness. These two faculties help you avoid gross forms of negative physical and verbal actions, deeds that are destructive for both oneself and others. Therefore, morality is the foundation of the Buddhist path.

The second phase is meditation, or training in higher concentration. When we talk about meditation in the general Buddhist sense, there are two principal types—absorptive and analytical. The first, absorptive meditation, refers primarily to the meditative states of tranquil abiding and the various meditative practices integrally associated with this state.[10] The main characteristics of this type of meditation are the feature of single-pointedness of mind and the absorptive quality that it generates. Analytical meditation, on the other hand, refers to meditative states that are more probing in terms of their mode of engagement with the object of meditation. It also includes the practices that are not characterized by mere single-pointedness of mind but are primarily associated with deeper analysis. Nevertheless, in both cases it is vital to have a stable foundation of mindfulness and alertness—faculties that originate, as we have seen, from a sound practice of ethical discipline. Even on the mundane level of our everyday life, the importance of mindfulness and alertness should not be underestimated.

To summarize, when we engage in the practice of morality, we lay the foundation for mental and spiritual development. When we engage in the complementary practice of concentration, we make the mind serviceable for and receptive to this higher purpose and prepare the mind for subsequent higher training in insight, or wisdom. With the faculty of single-pointedness that arises from concentration, we are able to channel all of our attention and mental energy towards a chosen object. Then, on the basis of a very stable state of mind, you can generate genuine insight into the ultimate nature of reality. Such penetrative insight into selflessness is the sole direct antidote to ignorance, as it alone is capable of eradicating our fundamental misknowing, or ignorance, together with the various deluded cognitive and afflictive emotional states arising from it.

THE THIRTY-SEVEN ASPECTS OF THE PATH TO ENLIGHTENMENT

The general structure of the Buddhist path is outlined in the first turning of the wheel of Dharma in terms of the thirty-seven aspects of the path to enlightenment. They are divided into seven categories. First are *the four mindfulnesses*, referring to mindfulness of body, feelings, mind, and phenomena.[11] *Mindfulness* here refers to contemplative practices that focus on the fundamentally unsatisfactory nature of samsara and on the transitoriness of this conditioned existence, the perpetual cycles of our habitual patterns of thought and behavior. It is by means of such reflections that the practitioner develops a true determination to become free from the cycle of conditioned existence.

Next are *the four complete abandonments.* These are so named because as practitioners develop a heart-felt determination to be free through their practice of the four mindfulnesses, they engage in a way of life in which they abandon the causes of future suffering and cultivate the causes of future happiness. Hence, the four abandonments are: (1) abandonment of unwholesome thoughts and actions already generated; (2) non-generation of unwholesome thoughts and actions not yet generated; (3) enhancement of wholesome thoughts and actions already generated; and (4) generation of wholesome thoughts and actions not yet generated.

Since you can overcome negative actions and their motivating afflictive emotions and increase the positive factors in your mind—technically called the class of pure phenomena—it is only when your mind is very concentrated that there follow what are known as *the four factors of miraculous powers.* These four factors are related to the practice of developing one's faculty of single-pointedness. They are also known as the four "legs" because they are the prerequisite factors that enable a practitioner to achieve the single-pointed states of mind that serve as the bases for supernatural manifestations. These four are the miraculous powers of aspiration, effort, intention, and analysis.

The fourth category consists of *the five faculties,* and the fifth category, of *the five powers.* In both categories, the list is identical: confidence, joyous effort, mindfulness, single-pointedness, and intelligence. In the present context, the distinction between a faculty and a power depends upon the practitioner's level of fluency in that particular skill; at a sufficiently advanced stage of fluency, a faculty becomes a power.

Next come *the seven branches of the path to enlightenment:* perfect mindfulness, perfect analysis, perfect effort, perfect joy, perfect pliancy, perfect meditative stabilization, and perfect equanimity.

The seventh and final category is *the noble eightfold path:* right view, right intention, right speech, right action, right livelihood, right effort, right mindfulness, and right meditative stabilization.

This, then, is the general structure of the Buddhist path as put forth in the first turning of the wheel of Dharma by the Buddha. Buddhism as practiced in the Tibetan tradition completely incorporates all these features of the Buddhist doctrine.

3

THE SECOND TURNING:
THE DOCTRINE OF EMPTINESS

IN THE SECOND TURNING of the wheel of Dharma at Vultures'
Peak,[12] the Buddha taught the wisdom sutras—the collection
of sutras known as perfection of wisdom (*prajñāpāramitā*). These
sutras focus primarily on the topics of emptiness and the transcendent states associated with the experience of emptiness.[13]
The second turning should be seen as expanding upon the topics
that the Buddha taught in the first turning of the wheel.

In the first turning, the Buddha taught the importance of rec-
ognizing the basic unsatisfactory nature of our own existence and
the suffering and pains that are integral to such a conditioned
existence. However, in the second turning, there is a major shift
in emphasis. Here, the practitioner is encouraged to expand the
scope of his or her contemplation on the nature of suffering so as
to encompass all other sentient beings. The second turning is,
therefore, much more extensive in its scope and vision.

Similarly, in terms of the treatment of the origin of suffering,
the second turning is much more comprehensive. In addition to
ignorance and attachment, the wisdom sutras identify in clear
detail various subtle forms of the delusions; these subtle forms
obstruct our ability to perceive reality in a manner untainted by
our habitual tendency to grasp at the inherent existence of all
phenomena. Hence, from this point of view, the origin of suffering is seen not only in the overt conscious factors of ignorance
and attachment but also in the subtle imprints and manifestations of these delusions.

Also, in the second turning, discussion of the third Noble Truth, true cessation, acquires greater profundity and complexity. Unlike the sutras belonging to the first turning, the teachings of the second turning go into great detail on the nature of cessation in general, its specific characteristics, and so forth.

This greater profundity and detail is also evident with regard to the presentation of the fourth Noble Truth, the true paths. With respect to the actual path to enlightenment, in the wisdom sutras the Buddha teaches a unique path based on generating a deep insight into emptiness, or selflessness, the true mode of being of all phenomena. This insight is cultivated on the basis of universal compassion and bodhicitta—the genuine altruistic aspiration to attain full enlightenment for the sake of all beings—attitudes which characterize a trainee of the Mahayana, or Universal Vehicle. The combination of insight into emptiness and realization of bodhicitta constitutes a perfect union of wisdom and skillful means. In this context, the factor of wisdom refers primarily to the experience of emptiness whereas the factor of method, or skillful means, refers primarily to the altruistic motive that directs this wisdom towards the fulfilment of one's compassionate ideals. This path of union is taught in the second turning of the wheel of Dharma.

Why is the presentation of the Four Noble Truths found in the second turning more profound than that found in the first? It is not merely because of the presence of some features that are taught in the wisdom sutras but are not found in the sutras of the first turning. This cannot be the reason. The point is this: the wisdom sutras not only discuss certain aspects of the Four Truths not covered in the first turning, but they also elaborate and develop the broader ramifications of the principle of causality that underlies the Four Truths, thus continuing the discussion at a more profound level. Moreover, this further development of the doctrine of the Four Truths takes place within the basic structure of the path as laid down in the first turning. It is on these grounds that I assert that the explanation found in the wisdom sutras pertaining to the doctrine of the Four Truths is more profound and comprehensive. Because of its extensive treatment of the topic of emptiness—the lack of intrinsic reality or intrinsic identity of all phenomena—the second turning of the wheel is known as "the wheel of Dharma pertaining to the absence of intrinsic characteristics."

Furthermore, in the discourses of the second turning, which are found in the wisdom sutras, we also find certain presentations that seem to contradict the general structure of the path as set forth in the first turning of the wheel. Because of this, in Mahayana Buddhism a distinction is made between two categories of scriptures: *interpretable* scriptures, which are those whose meaning can, at best, be taken as provisional and therefore require further interpretation beyond their literal meaning; and *definitive* scriptures, which are those scriptures that can be taken at face value as literally true. Crucial to this hermeneutical approach is the Mahayana principle of the four reliances. These are (1) reliance on the teaching, not on the teacher; (2) reliance on the meaning, not on the words that express it; (3) reliance on the definitive meaning, not on the provisional meaning; and (4) reliance on the transcendent wisdom of deep experience, not on mere knowledge.[14]

The first part of the principle of the four reliances states that when listening to a teaching or reading a text, one should not judge the validity of what is being said on the basis of the speaker's fame, wealth, position, or power but rather on the merit of the teaching itself. The second principle states that when judging a work, one should do so not on the basis of the literary style, but rather on the strength of the treatment of the subject matter. The third principle prescribes that when reflecting on the validity of a thesis, one should do so not on the strength of its provisional meaning but instead on the basis of its definitive stance. Finally, the fourth principle states that even when you rely on the definitive stance, you should do so based on the strength of wisdom and understanding gained through experience and not on mere intellectual knowledge of the subject matter. In fact, we can find indications of this approach in the Buddha's own words. He advises:

> O bhikṣus and wise men,
> Just as a goldsmith would test his gold
> By burning, cutting, and rubbing it,
> So must you examine my words and accept them.
> But not merely out of reverence for me.[15]

In essence, one can say that in the second turning of the wheel, as expounded in the sutras on the perfection of wisdom, the Buddha explores in great depth the subject of cessation in terms of an extensive discussion on the doctrine of emptiness. This hermeneutical approach also assists us in drawing out the implicit meanings of the various sutras. For example, we find that although the explicit subject matter of the wisdom sutras is the topic of emptiness, an implicit reading of the texts is also possible. According to the latter, the subject matter of the wisdom sutras then becomes the various levels of transcendent experience associated with the realization of emptiness: that is, the progressive stages of development along the path to enlightenment. This level of meaning is known as the hidden, or implicit, meaning of the wisdom sutras.

4

THE THIRD TURNING:
BUDDHA-NATURE

THE THIRD TURNING OF THE WHEEL OF DHARMA contains many different sutras, the most important being the *Tathā-gata Essence Sutra* (*Tathāgatagarbhasūtra*), which describes the innate potential for enlightenment that lies within us: our essence of buddhahood, or buddha-nature. This sutra is actually the source for Nāgārjuna's collection of hymns[16] and also Maitreya's treatise, the *Mahāyāna-uttaratantraśāstra* (*The Sublime Continuum of the Great Vehicle*).[17] In this sutra, the Buddha further explores the main topics he touched upon in the second turning, namely, the doctrine of emptiness and the transcendent experiences associated with its realization within the context of an individual's path to enlightenment. However, since the nature of emptiness itself—the emptiness of inherent existence of all phenomena—was already fully explained at its most subtle and profound level in the wisdom sutras, there is no subtler doctrine of emptiness expounded in the third turning. What is unique about the third turning is its presentation of particular meditative techniques aimed at enhancing the wisdom realizing emptiness and its discussion, from a subjective perspective, of the various subtle factors involved in a person's experience of that wisdom.

There is also another category of sutras belonging to the third turning of the wheel of Dharma. The main sutra in this category is the *Sutra Unravelling the Thought of the Buddha* (*Saṃdhinirmo-canasūtra*). In this sutra, the Buddha reconciles an apparent contradiction between certain statements in the first turning that ascribe intrinsic identity to phenomena and his explicit denial of intrinsic identity in the second turning. The Buddha does this by clarifying the doctrine of emptiness, or identitylessness, and showing how it must, in fact, be applied differently to different categories of phenomena. According to this view, existence is to be understood in terms of three classes: imputed phenomena, dependent phenomena, and thoroughly established, or ultimate, phenomena. *Imputed phenomena* refers to phenomena that exist only as concepts imputed in relation to other entities possessing a more autonomous reality. They include abstract entities, such as universals, relations, negative phenomena (such as the mere absence of something), and so on. *Dependent phenomena* refers to all things and events that come into being as the result of causes and conditions. The third category, *thoroughly established phenomena*, refers to the ultimate mode of being of all phenomena: emptiness.

From another perspective, the above three categories can also be seen as distinct but universal natures of all phenomena. In this view, they then become, respectively, the imputed nature, dependent nature, and thoroughly established nature. Corresponding to these three natures, different meanings are given to the term identitylessness. For example, imputed phenomena lack intrinsic identity, dependent phenomena lack identity derived from self-production, and thoroughly established phenomena lack ultimate identity.[18] Because of this, the third turning of the wheel is called "the wheel of Dharma clearly elucidating the distinctions."

This way of understanding the doctrine of identitylessness, as presented in the third turning, although at variance with the spirit of the wisdom sutras as expounded in the second turning, can be seen as exceptional skillful means on the part of the Buddha. In the second turning, the principle of identitylessness was described as a universal doctrine explicitly stated in terms of the emptiness of inherent existence of all phenomena. However, this view of emptiness may appear to be too extreme to many practitioners and thus remain beyond their scope of understanding. For these people, saying that phenomena lack inherent existence seems equivalent to saying that phenomena do not exist at all. In their minds, absence of inherent existence might equal non-existence. Hence, we can see that the Buddha taught the sutras of the third turning, such as the *Sutra Unravelling the Thought*, specifically in order to suit the mental faculties and dispositions of a particular type of practitioner. Based, respectively, on these two distinct systems of interpreting the doctrine of emptiness set forth in the wisdom sutras, there emerged in India the two major Mahayana schools of Buddhism: Middle Way, or *Madhyamaka*, and Mind Only, or *Cittamātra*.

In the Tibetan Buddhist tradition, there is also an advanced system of thought and practice known as tantra. I think this has some connection with the third turning of the wheel. The word *tantra* literally means *continuum*, or *lineage*. The Yoga Tantra text called the *Vajra-Pinnacle Tantra* (*Vajraśekharamahāguhyayogatantra*) explains that tantra is a continuity referring primarily to the continuity of mind or consciousness:

> "Tantra" is known as continuity:
> Samsara is considered as tantra.
> "Later" means beyond:
> Nirvana is the later tantra.[19]

In the first place, our mental continuum is the basis of our self-identity as a person. It is on the basis of this continuum that—on the ordinary level—we commit contaminated actions, which propel us round and round the vicious cycle of death and rebirth. On the spiritual path, it is also on the basis of this continuity of consciousness that we are able to make mental improvements and experience high realizations of the path. Finally, it is also on the basis of this same continuity of consciousness—which is often identified with our buddha-nature—that we are able to achieve the ultimate state of omniscience. In other words, samsara—our conditioned existence in the perpetual cycle of habitual tendencies—and nirvana—genuine freedom from such an existence—are nothing but different manifestations of this basic continuum. So, this continuity of consciousness is always present. This is the meaning of tantra, or continuity.

I feel there is close connection between the teachings of tantra and the Buddha's third turning of the wheel. As we can see, tantra is a system of thought and practice principally aimed at making manifest the dormant potentials of our basic continuity of consciousness, and this is also the ultimate aim of the teachings of the third turning.

In fact, if we examine carefully the teachings of the second and the third turnings, we can see significant features heralding the tantric path. Taken together, these two turnings provide a valuable bridge between the teachings of the sutras and the teachings of the tantras. For example, the hermeneutic principle of according two distinct readings to the wisdom sutras—that is, the explicit reading concerned with the doctrine of emptiness and the implicit reading showing the stages of the path associated with one's experience of emptiness—paves the way for acceptance of the idea of diverse interpretations of a single text, a crucial concept in understanding the tantric scriptures. Similarly, by touching upon the theme of varying levels of subtlety in one's experience of emptiness from the perspective of the subjective mind, the third turning opens the door for discussion, in tantra, of the many levels of subtlety in one's consciousness and their relevance to the actualization of various transcendent states.[20]

5

Different Explanations of Selflessness

FROM A PHILOSOPHICAL POINT OF VIEW, the criterion that distinguishes a school as Buddhist is its acceptance of four fundamental tenets, known as the four seals. These are:

> All composite phenomena are impermanent.
> All contaminated things and events are unsatisfactory.
> All phenomena are empty and selfless.
> Nirvana is true peace.

Any system accepting these four seals is philosophically a Buddhist school of thought. However, it is in the Mahayana schools (Cittamātra and Madhyamaka) that the principle of selflessness—the emptiness of self-existence—is explained at its most profound level.

As we have seen, there are two main approaches to the view of selflessness: the Hinayana and the Mahayana. The Hinayana, or Individual Vehicle, schools *(Vaibhāṣika* and *Sautrāntika)* adhere to the view of selflessness of the person as taught in the first turning, whereas the Mahayana schools adopt the more expansive view of selflessness indicated in the wisdom sutras taught in the second turning. In order to appreciate the difference in subtlety between these two views of selflessness, let us examine our own experiences and the ways in which we relate to others and to the world. For example, when I use this rosary by counting the beads or playing with it, I have a natural feeling that this is mine. There is a certain degree of grasping and attachment

31

based on this idea of "mineness." If you examine the attachment you feel for your possessions, you will find that there are different levels of attachment. Even our experience of a single emotional state, such as attachment, is composed of complex networks between various emotional and cognitive experiences. At one level, we feel as if there were a substantially existent, self-sufficient person. Such a person appears as totally independent, a separate entity from my body and mind, and the rosary is perceived as belonging to this unitary, fixed, and independent self, or "I." However, through meditation, when you begin to perceive the absence of such a self-sufficient, substantial person, you gradually begin to release the strong grip of your clinging toward friends and possessions. With this technique, you overcome strong and afflictive attachments by loosening your grip on your own fixed identity as a subject. This has a definitely liberating effect. Nevertheless, since this approach still leaves intact your apprehension of external objects as possessing an objective, intrinsic identity, subtle levels of attachment based on this apprehension also remain untouched. For example, when we see a beautiful flower, our habitual tendency is to project onto it qualities of beauty and goodness that exist in and of themselves and thus possess an objective status. Therefore, in the second turning of the wheel, the Buddha extends the principle of selflessness to encompass the entire expanse of reality, all things and events. Only by fully realizing the universal principle of emptiness can we overcome all levels of our deluded states of mind.

We can appreciate this point by reflecting on the following statement from Candrakīrti in his *Madhyamakāvatāra* (*Entering into the Middle Way*):

> The meditator who has realized the absence of a self [simply as the non-existence of an eternal self] would not comprehend the reality of form and the other [aggregates as expressed in the truth of the highest meaning]. On this account,

clinging and the other [afflictions] would still be
produced, for they arise through the [mis]appre-
hension of form, and he would not have compre-
hended the nature (i.e., the emptiness) of form
[and the other aggregates].[21]

In this passage, Candrakīrti is saying that the doctrine of selflessness as expounded in the lower, or Hinayana, schools of
Buddhist tenets is not complete, for according to these schools,
the principle is limited only to the person and thus is relevant only
in a discussion of personal identity. Moreover, this selflessness is
understood only in terms of the absence of a substantially existent
person possessing a distinct, self-sufficient identity. However, as
mentioned earlier, even when one achieves insight into this level
of selflessness, one is still unable to overcome the subtle clinging
to external objects and, hence, to one's own identity as well.

Although all Buddhist schools of thought accept the principle
of selflessness, there are major differences in their understanding
of the doctrine. Compared to the lower schools, the presentation
of selflessness in the higher schools of Buddhist thought is more
profound. The realization of selflessness as understood by the
lower schools does not constitute a full realization of the principle. The reason is that even though one may have realized the
person as lacking self-sufficient and substantial existence, this
still leaves room for grasping at one's own self as possessing
intrinsic identity, or being inherently existent. On the other
hand, if one has realized the absence of intrinsic identity of the
person—that the person totally lacks any form of independent
nature or inherent existence—this precludes the possibility of
apprehending the person as a self-sufficient entity.

Given that the negation of self-identity—in the context of an
understanding of emptiness—is much more radical in the presentation of the higher schools, the ascertainment of selflessness in
accord with such a view naturally acquires a greater power to

counteract both the delusions and the underlying misconception that apprehends phenomena as inherently existent and grasps onto that as true. However, it must be pointed out that the doctrine of emptiness in no way refutes the conventional existence of phenomena: the reality of our conventional world, within the framework of which all functions of reality—such as causation, relation, negation, and so forth—validly operate, is left unscathed and intact. What is demolished is the reified fiction that has resulted from our habitual tendency to grasp at phenomena as self-existent.

These divergent views in the various schools on the nature of selflessness must all be perceived within a coherent system: one view progressively leads to the next, as one step on a staircase naturally leads to the next. This understanding becomes possible if the different views of selflessness are examined against the background of the fundamental Buddhist principle of dependent origination. In the present context, dependent origination refers to the principle of interdependence that governs the relationship between causes and their results, especially those that effect our experience of suffering and happiness. In the classical literature, this principle is explained in terms of the twelve links of dependent origination.[22] Together, these twelve links form the factors that complete one instance of birth in a karmically conditioned existence, or in other words, in samsara. The principle of dependent origination is fundamental to the Buddhist worldview, and any interpretation of the doctrine of selflessness that fails to perceive emptiness in terms of dependent origination can never be complete. In fact, the subtler your negation (of true existence) becomes, the stronger should be your conviction about the efficacy of the relative world. In essence, a genuine realization of emptiness reaffirms your conviction about the interdependent nature of things and events, and this understanding of interdependence further reinforces your ascertainment of the emptiness of all phenomena.

However, since people have diverse mental dispositions with differing interests, levels of intelligence, and so on, the view of emptiness as defined above—the emptiness of inherent existence—may not suit the mentality of all trainees. It is possible that, for some, the absence of inherent existence would literally mean non-existence. Should this happen, there is the grave danger that one will fall into the extreme of nihilism. In view of this danger, the Buddha also taught less subtle views of selflessness that can skillfully lead the practitioner to an eventual appreciation of the subtlest doctrine of emptiness. If we subject the views of the higher schools to analysis from the viewpoint of the lower schools, no contradiction or logical inconsistencies can be found within the tenets of the higher schools. On the contrary, if we examine the various tenets of the lower schools from the philosophical standpoint of the higher schools, certain untenable premises and inconsistencies can be observed within the positions of the lower schools.

6

THE FOUR SEALS OF BUDDHISM

THE FOUR SEALS, axioms that are common to all schools of Buddhism, have a profound significance for the practitioner. As explained earlier, the first seal states that all composite phenomena are impermanent. The nature of impermanence is explored to its fullest extent in the tenets of the Sautrāntika school. According to this view, all composite phenomena are impermanent in that they are momentary: the very conditions that brought them into being also cause their disintegration. Any thing or event that comes into being as a result of other factors does not require a secondary condition for its disintegration. The moment it comes into existence, the process of disintegration has already begun. In other words, the mechanism for cessation is built into the system itself. It is as if things and events carry the seed of their own eventual demise. The simple reason is that anything that is produced through causes is other-powered: its very existence comes about only in dependence upon other factors. This Buddhist view of phenomena as dynamic and of momentary nature—which emerges as a consequence of the principle of universal impermanence—is quite close to the view of a dynamic, ever-changing physical universe as presented by modern physics.

The second seal states that all contaminated phenomena are, by nature, unsatisfactory. In this context, *contaminated phenomena* refers to all things, events, experiences, and so forth, that are products of contaminated actions and the underlying delusions that give rise to them. As explained earlier, anything that is produced is other-powered, in the sense that it is under the control of factors other than itself—for example, its causes and conditions. Here, *causes* specifically refers to our own fundamental ignorance, afflictive emotions and cognitive events, and contaminated actions. Also, ignorance must not be perceived as a passive state of mere non-awareness; rather, it is a deluded state of mind, a fundamental misapprehension of the nature of reality. This is clearly stated by various Indian masters, such as Dharmakīrti and Vasubandhu. Vasubandhu tells us in his *Abhidharmakośa* (*Treasury of Knowledge*) that ignorance is not simply the absence of knowledge but rather it is the antithesis of knowledge; it is misknowledge, a force actively opposing knowledge, as hostility opposes friendliness and falsehood opposes truth.[23]

As long as beings are under the control of these forces of ignorance, suffering and unsatisfactoriness will always remain integral parts of their mode of being. And we should not think that suffering, or *duḥkha*, refers only to manifest physical and mental suffering; it is extremely important that we remember that the underlying experiences of discomfort and dissatisfaction are also duḥkha.

By contemplating these two marks of conditioned existence—impermanence and duḥkha—one can develop genuine renunciation, a deeply felt spontaneous wish to be free from the bondage of suffering. The question then arises, is it possible for an individual to attain such a state of freedom? This is where the significance of the third seal becomes evident. The third principle states that all phenomena are empty of self-existence. The path from impermanence and unsatisfactoriness to selflessness is quite clear. We learned from the principle of dependent origination that things and events do not come into being without causes. We also noted that suffering and unsatisfactory conditions are caused by our own delusions and the contaminated actions induced by them. The underlying root of all delusions is the fundamental ignorance misapprehending the nature of reality. This ignorance is a state of misconception. Since it misapprehends the nature of reality, it has no valid grounding in our experience or in reality. In fact, it apprehends reality in a manner contradictory to the way things actually are. Hence, it is an erroneous and distorted state of mind. As this is so, it opens up for us the real possibility of eradicating it. We can accomplish this by generating the insight that can penetrate the illusion created by this misconception. True cessation is the state that is free from this distorted way of perceiving the world. It is an actuality that you can bring about within your own mental continuum. It is not a mere ideal. The nature of cessation is true peace. Hence, the fourth principle—nirvana is true peace—is also directly relevant to your practice.

7

THE MAHAYANA PATH OF EMPTINESS AND COMPASSION

READING MAHAYANA SCRIPTURES: THE DEFINITIVE AND THE INTERPRETABLE

WHEN WE REFLECT ON THE CONCEPTS explained earlier, we find that the first teaching given by the Buddha on the Four Noble Truths is like a presentation of a master plan of the entire Buddhist doctrine, and that when we take into account all the different explanations of the various philosophical schools within Buddhism, including Mahayana, it becomes necessary to distinguish between the various sutras: some are definitive, and others require further interpretation. If we make these distinctions on the basis of a particular scriptural text, or sutra, we need another scriptural text to actually determine whether that guiding text itself is definitive or not. Then, we require yet another sutra to determine the validity of that one. Thus, the process continues infinitely and has no benefit as a criterion. Furthermore, different sutras propound contrasting methods of discriminating between the definitive and interpretive meanings. In the end, one must determine whether a sutra is definitive or interpretable on the basis of reason. Therefore, we can see that from the perspective of Mahayana tradition, reason becomes more important than scripture.

How do we determine if a particular expression or text is interpretable? There are different types of scriptures that belong to this category. For instance, in certain sutras it is said that one must kill one's parents. Now, since these sutras cannot be taken literally or at face value, they require further interpretation. *Parents* here refers to contaminated actions and attachment, which result in future rebirth.

Similar statements can be found also in the tantras, such as the *Guhyasamāja Tantra*, wherein the Buddha says that the Tathāgata—the Buddha—is to be killed, and that by killing the Buddha, you will be able to achieve supreme enlightenment.[24] Surely such admonitions cannot be accepted as literal!

Then there are other types of interpretable scriptures. For instance, the sutra explaining the twelve links of dependent origination says that if the cause exists, the fruits will ensue. So, for example, if there is ignorance in one's mind, contaminated actions will follow.

> Due to the existence of this, that arises.
> Due to the production of this, that is engendered.
> It is thus: due to ignorance, there is the volitional action;
> Due to action, there is consciousness...[25]

These types of sutras, which seem literal—because the above statement is certainly true—are categorized as interpretable in that the ignorance that induces contaminated actions is referred to here from the conventional point of view, wherein something can produce something else. However, on the ultimate level, its nature is emptiness. There is thus a further, deeper level of reality not referred to in this sutra. Therefore, it is again said to be interpretable.

The definitive sutras are the wisdom sutras, such as the *Heart of Wisdom* (*Prajñāpāramitāhṛdaya*),[26] in which the Buddha spoke of the ultimate nature of all phenomena: that form is emptiness and emptiness is form, and apart from form, there is no emptiness. Because such sutras speak of the ultimate nature of all phenomena—that is, their empty nature, or mode of existence—they are said to be definitive. The class of definitive scriptures also includes the *Tathāgata Essence Sutra* from the third turning of the wheel. As mentioned previously, this is the scriptural source for Maitreya's *Uttaratantra* and Nāgārjuna's collection of praises.

One should, however, also take into account the fact that the different Buddhist schools employ various means of discriminating between the interpretable and definitive sutras. In brief, the writings of the Prāsaṅgika sub-school of the Madhyamaka school—especially those of Nāgārjuna and his follower Candrakīrti—are the most reliable. They explain to the fullest extent the ultimate view of emptiness as taught by the Buddha. The view of emptiness expounded by them does not contradict valid analysis or experience on the one hand, and has the support of logical reasoning on the other.

The proponents of the *Shen-tong*, or emptiness of other, view accept only ten sutras as definitive, all of which belong to the third turning.[27] This school maintains that conventional phenomena are empty of themselves, and that all phenomena are ultimately empty of existing even conventionally. One could interpret this view of emptiness—that sees conventional phenomena as being empty of themselves—in the following way: phenomena are conventional because they are not their own ultimate nature. In that sense, they are empty of themselves. However, many Tibetan scholars who subscribe to the Shen-tong view do not interpret emptiness in such a manner. Rather, they maintain that if phenomena are empty of themselves, that is, of their conventionality, they cannot exist at all.

As we can read from history, many masters belonging to this group actually achieved high realizations on the Generation and Completion Stages of tantra. Since they must have achieved these realizations by means of the practice of meditation conjoined with their own view of emptiness, it would seem that they must have achieved some profound understanding or interpretation of their particular view of emptiness. However, if we were to understand their view—that things are empty of themselves—as literally signifying that things do not exist, then this would be tantamount to asserting that nothing exists at all! This, then, would constitute falling into the extreme of nihilism. This consequence, in my view, arises because of an inability on the part of Shen-tong proponents to accept an identity and existence of phenomena that derives from a mere dependence on others. That they maintain the literal meaning—that conventional phenomena do not exist and are empty of themselves—becomes clear when we examine their position on the ontological status attributed to ultimate truth. They maintain that ultimate nature is a truly existent phenomenon, existing inherently and in its own right. So when they speak of the emptiness of this ultimate natural truth, they are saying that ultimate truth is empty of conventional phenomena.

Dharmeśvara, the spiritual son of Yungmo Mikyö Dorje—one of the founders and the foremost proponent of this view—asserts in one of his writings that Nāgārjuna's view of emptiness is a nihilistic view. In Dharmeśvara's own view, because conventional phenomena are empty of themselves, the only thing that exists is ultimate truth, and that ultimate truth exists truly and inherently, as an objective entity.

It becomes obvious that adherence to such a philosophical viewpoint directly contradicts the view of emptiness as explained in the *Perfection of Wisdom*, or wisdom sutras. There, the Buddha explicitly and clearly mentioned that in the sphere of emptiness, there is no distinction whatsoever between conventional phenomena and ultimate phenomena. He expounded the empty nature of ultimate phenomena by using different synonyms for ultimate truth[28] and established as a part of his fundamental teaching on emptiness that all phenomena, ranging from form up to omniscience,[29] are equal in being empty.

THE PROFOUND VIEW

Although the proponents of the Prāsaṅgika view—the highest philosophical school of tenets—speak of phenomena as being

44

empty and as having an empty nature, this is not to be misinterpreted as implying that phenomena do not exist at all. Rather, phenomena do not exist by themselves, in and of themselves, in their own right, or inherently. Because phenomena possess the characteristics of existing and occurring and are dependent on other factors—causes, conditions, and so forth—they are, therefore, devoid of an independent nature. Consequently, they have the nature of being dependent. The very fact that they have this nature of dependence—being dependent on other factors—is an indication that they lack an independent status. When Madhyamaka-Prāsaṅgika proponents speak of emptiness, they speak of the empty nature of phenomena in terms of dependent origination. Therefore, an understanding of emptiness does not contradict the conventional reality of phenomena.

To establish the empty nature of phenomena, the Prāsaṅgikas cite, as their ultimate and conclusive reason, the dependent nature of phenomena. They reason that because phenomena come into being and exist in dependence on other factors, they lack an independent nature. Hence, they are devoid of intrinsic reality and identity. This manner of coming to the view of emptiness through the reasoning of dependent origination is very profound, because it not only dispels the misconception of apprehending phenomena as inherently existent, but at the same time, it protects the person from falling into the extreme of nihilism.

In Nāgārjuna's own writings, we find statements that emptiness must be understood in terms of dependent origination. In his *Mūlamadhyamakakārikā* (*Fundamentals of the Middle Way*), Nāgārjuna says that in a system where emptiness is not possible, nothing is possible. In a system where emptiness is possible, however, everything is possible.[30] Another passage states, "Since there is no phenomenon that does not arise through dependence, there is no phenomenon that is not empty."[31]

Nāgārjuna's view of emptiness must be understood in the context of dependent origination. This is not only clear in Nāgārjuna's own writings, but also in the later commentaries, such as the lucid, concise text composed by Buddhapālita, and in the writings of Candrakīrti—particularly in his commentary on *Madhyamakakārikā* called *Prasannapadā* (*Clear Words*) and in his *Madhyamakāvatāra* (*Guide to the Middle Way*), as well as in his autocommentary to that text.[32] There also exists a commentary by Candrakīrti on Āryadeva's *Catuḥśataka-śāstrakārikā* (*Four Hundred Verses*). If you undertake a comparative study of all these texts, it becomes very clear that the view of emptiness as expounded by Nāgārjuna must be understood in terms of dependent origination. When you read these commentaries, you begin to develop great admiration for Nāgārjuna.

This, in brief, is an overview of the Buddhist path as presented in the teachings of the Buddhist sutras.

8

QUESTIONS AND ANSWERS

Q: HOW DOES ONE ARRIVE at the conviction that our consciousness has no beginning or end, or is this just a question of faith?

HHDL: There are two ways of developing this conviction. One is by examining the reasons that establish the validity of this view by means of a logical process, such that we are led to this conclusion. This is one way of generating conviction about a certain phenomenon. With other types of phenomena, you may not be able to arrive at a certain conclusion by means of direct logical reasoning that establishes and supports its validity. Here, you can examine the premise by adopting a contrary viewpoint and see whether this opposing thesis entails any inherent inconsistencies or logical contradictions. By doing this, you may find mysterious elements in your view that cannot be explained. Since this contrary position contains many inconsistencies, you can arrive at the conclusion that it must be the other way around!

On this question, I think it is also important to understand that, generally speaking, there are three categories of phenomena. *Manifest phenomena* are those that can be directly observed. *Slightly obscure phenomena* are those that can be inferred through a process of reasoning. Third, there are *very obscure phenomena*, which remain beyond ordinary direct perception and logical inference. Generally speaking, the existence of these very obscure phenomena can be established only on the basis of another's testimony and on scriptural authority.

In addition, we should understand that in Buddhism there

are four different ways of examining these different categories of phenomena known as the *four principles*. The first is the *principle of reality*. For example, our consciousness is in the nature of luminosity and knowing. Why is it of such a nature? There is no reason; this is just its nature. Similarly, our physical body is composed of atoms and chemical particles. This too is simply its nature, the way it is. Next is the *principle of dependence*. This refers to phenomena that are posited in relation to something else, for example, parts and the whole, right and wrong, and so on.

The third principle is the *principle of efficacy*. This includes phenomena such as causes, whose function is to produce an effect, and effects, which function by following after their related causes. Lastly, the *principle of valid proof* comprises the rules of logic—ascertainable on the basis of the three preceding principles—that govern the relationships between various entities and, thereby, enable us to generate inferences from valid premises.[33]

The approach entailed in the fourfold analysis just described is quite similar to the basic approach of science. For instance, the principle of reality is, in some aspects, similar to certain theories of subatomic physics concerning the nature of particles. There are passages in the *Kālacakra Tantra* that explain that space particles, or particles composed of space, are the source of all matter in the universe. In a similar way, there is a close parallel between the operation of the second principle and the laws of chemistry. At the subatomic level, we find the principle of reality at work. When these particles aggregate, coming together to form objects and interacting with other types of particles, we find the principle of dependence at work. Then again, when there is an interaction of different types of chemical particles, resulting in different emergent properties, this is very similar to the third principle, the principle of efficacy. Taking these three principles of relationship between phenomena as the basis of analysis, we can employ the rules of logical reasoning embodied in the fourth principle.

In the context of this question about the beginningless continuity of consciousness, if we adhere to the opposite position, that there is a beginning somewhere, then a big question mark appears. How did that first moment of consciousness come into being? Where did it come from? There are many logical contradictions and inconsistencies that arise in positing a starting point. A person adhering to this position must either accept that the first moment arises from no cause at all or accept the existence of a creator.

Any instance of consciousness requires a substantial cause in the form of another preceding moment of consciousness. Because of this, we maintain that consciousness is infinite and beginningless. This position seems to have fewer contradictions. Although this kind of explanation may not give you 100 percent satisfaction, you can still quite safely conclude that such a position contains fewer contradictions and has fewer logical inconsistencies, and based on this, you can generate conviction about it.

Q: If the phenomena that I perceive are projections of my own mind, then why do we all perceive the same phenomena as the same thing? I see a text wrapped in an orange cloth in front of Your Holiness. Why does everyone else see it as that also? Further, I have read that beings of the other five worlds perceive these phenomena as different things, but that they still share a common perception. Why?

HHDL: According to the explanation of the highest Buddhist philosophical school, Madhyamaka-Prāsaṅgika, external phenomena are not mere projections or creations of the mind. External phenomena have a distinct nature, which is different from the mind. The meaning of all phenomena being mere labels or designations is that they exist and acquire their identities by means of our denomination or designation of them. This does not mean that there is no phenomenon apart from the name, imputation, or label, but rather that if we analyze and search objectively for the essence of any phenomenon, it will be unfindable. Phenomena are unable to withstand such analysis; therefore, they do not exist objectively. Yet since they exist, there should be some level of existence; therefore, it is only through our own process of labeling or designation that things are said to exist.

Since phenomena have no independent, objective reality, there is no status of existence from the side of the object; therefore, we conclude that phenomena exist only nominally, or conventionally. However, when things appear to us, they do not appear as mere designations; rather, they appear to us as if they have some kind of objective reality or inherent existence "out there." Thus, there is a disparity between the way things appear to us and the way they exist. This is why they are said to be illusory.

The actual mode of existence of phenomena can be ascertained only through your own experience, once you have negated their inherent existence. But conventional reality cannot be logically proven. For example, this table exists because we can touch it, feel it, put things on it, and so on; thus, it exists. It is only through our direct experience of a phenomenon that we can establish the reality of its existence.

The Prāsaṅgikas speak of three criteria that determine whether or not something is existent: (1) it should be known through a worldly convention; (2) such a convention should not be contradicted by any form of validation; and (3) it should not be contradicted by an ultimate analysis of its nature. Anything possessing these three criteria is said to be conventionally existent.[34]

There are many different types of perception that can apprehend a single object, such as the cloth wrapping around this text. For many people it appears as orange, but for some, the color orange may not appear because of illness or other physiological conditions, such as in the case of those who suffer from color blindness. Other beings, because of their karma, would also not be able to see this cloth as orange in the way that we do.

Q: Your Holiness, as the recognized reincarnation of the Thirteenth Dalai Lama, and therefore presumably possessing the same mindstream, perhaps you could explain for what purpose you, as a realized being, had to go through various schools of training and take examinations, and so on, when your knowledge of these things could be likened to a skilled mechanic learning basic car maintenance again!

HHDL: I could not have acquired my present level of knowledge without engaging in serious study, so I had to study. This is a reality, and there is no point in pretending otherwise. Perhaps there were a few occasions when I found I could understand, without much effort and hardship, certain philosophical points that are normally considered difficult. In relatively little time and with little effort I am usually able to understand difficult subjects. This indicates that perhaps in my past lives I may have pursued some studies. Otherwise, I am just an ordinary person, like you—so that is that!

Q: Could Your Holiness explain the meaning of the terms *imputation* and *basis of imputation*? Could you also indicate how the lower and higher Buddhist schools differ in their understanding of imputation and basis of imputation?

HHDL: Except for the Prāsaṅgika school, all the other Buddhist schools of thought identify the existence of phenomena within the basis of designation; therefore, they maintain that there is some kind of objective existence.

For example, when the lower schools identify the person, or self, they identify it as the continuity of consciousness. But according to Buddhist literature belonging to the higher schools, this kind of philosophical viewpoint leads to contradiction or inconsistency when we speak about unconscious states of meditation. Other contradictions also arise when the individual has reached the high attainment of what is known as *uncontaminated wisdom*, during which it becomes problematic to identify the person with the continuity of consciousness.

Since the lower schools of Buddhist thought all accept that things exist inherently, they assert some kind of objective existence, maintaining that things exist in their own right and from their own side. This is because they identify phenomena within the basis of designation. For the Prāsaṅgikas, if anything exists objectively and is identified within the basis of designation, then that is, in fact, equivalent to saying that it exists autonomously, that it has an independent nature and exists in its own right. At this point, we should consider the nature of dependence. It is obvious in many cases that many phenomena cannot be posited without depending on other factors. When we analyze and search for the essence, the true referent behind the labels, things disintegrate, and we cannot find something that is that essence. Rather, we find that *something* exists, but that it exists by the force of or depending on other factors, and these other factors include, most importantly, our own imputation, the process of labeling. This is why the Prāsaṅgikas say that there is no objective reality or inherent existence.

Let us consider, for example, *present* time. It is definite that the present exists, but let's examine what it is in greater depth. We can divide time: the time that is gone is the *past*, and the time that is yet to come is the *future*. If we divide time even more minutely, we will find that there is hardly anything remaining that we can truly call present. We find that between the past and the future there is an extremely thin line—something that cannot really withstand analysis and remain as the *present*. If we were to maintain a single point in time as indivisible, then there would be no grounds for dividing between the past, present, and future, because it would all be indivisible. But when we speak of divisible time, then there is hardly any *present* remaining between the past and future.

If the present cannot be posited, how can past and future be posited? Past is called past in relation to the present, and future is called future in relation to the present as well. If we were to conclude that the present does not exist, this would contradict worldly convention and our everyday thought and experience as well as many other facts. Therefore, we can say that the present does exist, but not inherently or objectively. This is a demonstration of dependent origination.

Q: In the *Pramāṇavārttika* (*Commentary on the Compendium of Valid Cognition*), Dharmakīrti says that since the object of cognition is invariably experienced together with its cognitive image, how can an object of cognition be established as distinct from its cognitive image? Could Your Holiness please comment on this, especially with regard to any significance this might have for Generation Stage practice in tantra?

HHDL: In this passage, Dharmakīrti is talking about what is known as the argument of *constant co-cognition*. This is a philosophical tenet of the Yogācāra school in which external reality is negated, that is, the atomically structured external world is negated. Because the proponents of the Yogācāra philosophical system assert that things cannot exist other than as projections of one's own mind, they also maintain that there is no atomically structured external physical reality independent of mind.

As we read in the *Viṃśatikā* (*Twenty Verses*),[35] Vasubandhu takes the so-called indivisible atom postulated by the Realist schools and examines it critically. He suggests that we try to imagine an indivisible atom that has no directional parts at all. But if something is matter, it cannot be indivisible, because matter has the defining characteristic of being obstructive and, therefore, has directional parts. Consequently, it cannot be indivisible. By analyzing along these lines, Yogācāra proponents conclude that there is no atomically structured external reality. This conclusion is reached because of not having understood the most subtle level of emptiness as expounded by the Prāsaṅgikas. In fact, Yogācārins assert that things have inherent existence, and that if you analyze something and do not find any essence, then it does not exist at all. Prāsaṅgikas, on the other hand, when confronted with this unfindability of the essence of the object, conclude that this is an indication that objects do not exist inherently, not that they do not exist at all. This is where the difference lies between the two schools.

Q: Certain tantric texts mention eight types of consciousness?

HHDL: When eight types of consciousness are mentioned, it includes the fundamental consciousness. The fundamental consciousness referred to here is completely different from the fundamental consciousness found in the writings of the Yogācāra school. The fundamental consciousness in Highest Yoga Tantra can be generated into the wisdom realizing emptiness; therefore, it is synonymous with the fundamental innate mind of clear light. The fundamental, or foundational, consciousness referred to by the Yogācāra school is always neutral—that is, neither virtuous nor non-virtuous in nature.

There are, however, Indian masters, such as Śāntipāda and Abhayākara, who, while adhering to a philosophical system that negates the existence of atomically structured external reality, have attained high realizations of tantra. The tradition maintains that when they first engaged in the practice of tantra, these masters were proponents of Yogācāra or Madhyamaka-Svātantrika-Yogācāra. Later, as a result of their high realizations on the tantric path, they were able to realize profound emptiness as propounded by the Prāsaṅgikas.

Therefore, when you undertake the practice of the Generation

Stage of tantra, if possible and if it suits your mental faculty, it is best to try to adhere to the Prasaṅgika view of emptiness right from the beginning. That is how most of the great masters and meditators of the past have progressed. The Prāsaṅgika system possesses the least number of logical inconsistencies and contradictions and the highest level of validity.

Candrakīrti, in his commentary on the *Catuḥśataka* by Āryadeva, strongly criticizes Dharmapāla, who interpreted the ultimate philosophical position of Āryadeva as being that of the Yogācāra school. In Candrakīrti's autocommentary to his *Madhyamakāvatāra* we also find this question: "Would you say that masters such as Vasubandhu, Dharmapāla, and the like have rejected the subtle view of emptiness due to their fear of the profound doctrine of the emptiness of inherent existence?" Candrakīrti replies with an emphatic "Yes!"

Thus, practitioners like myself—who appreciate the philosophical system expounded by Candrakīrti, and who praise Candrakīrti to such heights that his two treatises, the commentary on the *Guhyasamāja Tantra* and the one on *Mūlamadhayamaka*, are likened to the sun and moon—can definitely always follow Candrakīrti's example and say that yes, masters like Vasubandhu and Dharmapāla have rejected the profound view of emptiness.

PART II

An Altruistic Outlook
and Way of Life

9

THE BENEFITS OF ALTRUISM

THE DIVERSE TEACHINGS OF THE BUDDHA all outline various methods for training and transforming the mind. Historically, however, a traditional classification of certain practices, and the literature specifically associated with them, developed in Tibet and was known as lo-jong, which means mind training, or thought transformation. These practices and the related literature are so called because they aim at nothing short of bringing about a radical transformation in our thinking, and through it, our way of life. One of the principal characteristics of lo-jong practice is the overwhelming emphasis it places on overcoming our grasping at a solid ego identity and the self-cherishing attitudes based on this apprehension of self. The self-cherishing attitude obstructs us from generating genuine empathy towards others and limits our outlook to the narrow confines of our own self-centered concerns. In essence, with thought transformation, we seek to transform our normal selfish outlook on life into a more altruistic one, which, at the very least, regards the welfare of others as equal in importance to our own, and ideally regards others' welfare as much more important than ours.

The *Bodhicaryāvatāra*[36] by Śāntideva is the primary source of most all the literature belonging to this category. I received an oral transmission of this text from the late Kunu Lama Rinpoche. I myself try to apply this practice as much as possible and also, whenever the opportunity arises, explain it to others. During these three days together, as part of our discussion on Buddhist thought and practice, I would like to explore some of the main points of the practice of altruism as explained in chapters 6 and 8 of the text, which address the subjects of tolerance and meditation, respectively.

First, I will talk about the benefits of altruism and the good heart. A good heart is the true source of all happiness, not just in religious terms but also in our everyday life experience. As human beings, we are singularly social animals. Because of this basic nature, we are only able to survive in dependence upon the cooperation, help, and kindness of other fellow humans. This fact may become more evident if we reflect on the basic pattern of our existence. In order to do more than just barely survive, we need shelter, food, companions, friends, the esteem of others, resources, and so on; these factors do not come about from ourselves alone but are all dependent on others. Suppose one single person were to live alone in a remote and uninhabited place. No matter how strong, healthy, or educated the person were, there would be no possibility of his or her leading a happy and fulfilling existence. If a person is living, for example, somewhere deep in the African forest and is the only human being in an animal sanctuary, given that person's intelligence and cunning, the best he or she can do is to become, perhaps, king of the jungle. Can such a person have friends? Acquire renown? No matter how strong and healthy, can this person become a hero if he or she wishes to become one? I think the answer to all these questions is a definite "no," for all these factors come about only in relation to other fellow humans.

Even from a totally selfish perspective—wanting only our own happiness, comfort, and satisfaction in life, with no consideration of others' welfare or the welfare of our own possible future lives—I would still argue that the fulfillment of our aspirations requires dependence upon others. This is an indisputable fact. Even to commit unwholesome actions depends on the existence of others. For example, in order to cheat, you need someone as the object of your act. All events and incidents in life are so intimately linked with the fate of others that a single person on his own cannot even begin to act. Many ordinary human activities, both positive and negative, cannot even be conceived of apart from the existence of other people. Because of others, we have the opportunity to earn money if that is what we desire in life. Similarly, in reliance upon the existence of others it becomes possible for the media to create fame or disrepute for someone. A solitary person on his own cannot create any fame or disrepute no matter how loud he might shout. The closest he can get is to create an echo of his own voice.

As human beings, we have a natural tendency to appreciate the affection and cooperation of others. I learned from meeting with some scientists, especially those working in the field of neurobiology, that there is strong scientific evidence to suggest that even in pregnancy a mother's state of mind has a great effect on the physical and mental well-being of the unborn child. It seems vital for the mother to maintain a calm and relaxed state of mind. After parturition, the first few weeks are the most crucial period for the healthy development of the child. During this time, I was told, one of the most important factors for ensuring rapid and healthy growth of the baby's brain is the mother's constant physical touch. If the child is left unattended and uncared for during this critical period, although the effects on the child's mental well-being may not be immediately obvious, physical damage can result from this that will later become quite noticeable. When a child sees someone with an open and affectionate demeanor, someone who is smiling or has a loving and caring expression, the child naturally feels happy and protected. On the other hand, if someone tries to hurt the child, it becomes gripped by fear, which leads to harmful consequences in terms of the child's development. This is how our life begins.

When you are young, healthy, and strong, you sometimes get the feeling that you are totally independent and do not need anyone. But this is an illusion. Even at that prime age of your life, as a human being, you need friends, don't you? This is especially true when we become old. For example, in my own case, the Dalai Lama who is now in his fifties is beginning to show various signs of appoaching old age. I can see the appearance of more white hair on my head, and I am also starting to experience slight problems sometimes with the knees when getting up or sitting down. As we grow old, we need to rely more and more on the help of others: this is the nature of our lives as human beings. In human life, companions and friends are very important for sustaining happiness and satisfaction. Hence, the question of how to develop good friendships and relationships with one's companions assumes great importance. On a superficial level, you can "buy" friends; but in reality, these are friends of money and wealth. As long as you have money and wealth, these friends will be around, but as soon as your fortune declines, they will be all too happy to say good-bye to you. When this happens, there will be no more news from these so-called friends. They will have disappeared somewhere; they will have gone to find someone else who has more wealth. Clearly, the time when you most need a friend is when you are passing through a difficult stage in life. So, someone who disappears at that time is not a true friend. A person who still remains a friend, a support, when you are passing through a difficult period, is a genuine friend.

Now to reiterate the question, how do we make friends? Certainly not through hatred and confrontation. It is impossible to make friends by hitting people and fighting with them. A genuine friendship can emerge only through cooperation based on honesty and sincerity, and this means having an open mind and a warm heart. This, I think, is obvious from our own everyday interactions with others.

The need for such an atmosphere of openness and cooperation is also becoming more urgent at the global level. In this modern age, there are no longer family, or even national, boundaries when it comes to dealing with economic situations. From country to country and continent to continent, the world is inextricably interconnected. Each one depends heavily on the others. In order for a country to develop its own economy, it is forced to take seriously into account the economic conditions of other countries as well. In fact, economic improvement in other countries will ultimately result in economic improvement in one's own country. In view of these facts about our modern world, we need a total revolution in our thinking and our habits. It is becoming clearer every day that a viable economic system must be based on a true sense of universal responsibility. In other words, what we need is a genuine commitment to the principles of universal brotherhood and sisterhood. This much is clear, isn't it? This is not just a holy, moral, or religious ideal. Rather, it is the reality of our modern human existence.

If you reflect deeply enough, it becomes obvious that we need more compassion and altruism everywhere. This critical point can be appreciated from the current state of affairs in the world, whether in the fields of modern economics and health care, or as seen in the current political and military situations all over the world. In addition to the multitude of social and political crises, the world is also facing an ever-increasing cycle of natural calamities. Year after year, we have witnessed a radical shifting of global climatic patterns that has led to grave consequences in various parts of the world: excessive rain in some countries that has brought serious flooding, a shortage of precipitation in other countries that has resulted in devastating droughts. Fortunately, concern for ecology and the environment is rapidly growing everywhere. We are now beginning to appreciate that the question of environmental protection is ultimately a question of our very survival on this planet. As human beings, we must also respect our fellow members of the human family: our neighbors, our friends, and so forth. Compassion, loving kindness, altruism, and a sense of brotherhood and sisterhood are the keys to human development, not only in the future but in the present as well.

In simple terms, compassion and love can be defined as positive thoughts and feelings that give rise to such essential things in life as hope, courage, determination, and inner strength. The success or failure of humanity in the future depends primarily upon the will and determination of the present generation. If we ourselves do not utilize our faculties of will and human intelligence, no one else can guarantee our future and that of the next generation. This is an indisputable fact. We cannot place the entire blame on politicians or those people who are seen as directly responsible for various situations; we too must bear some responsibility. It is only when the individual accepts personal responsibility that he or she begins to take some initiative. Just shouting and making complaints is not good enough. A genuine change must first come from within the individual, then he or she can attempt to make significant contributions to humanity. Altruism is not merely a religious ideal; it is an indispensable requirement for humanity at large. Is that clear? Do you have any qualms about this?

The next question is whether or not it is possible to enhance compassion and altruism. In other words, is there a means by which these qualities of mind can be increased, and anger, hatred, and jealousy reduced? The answer to this is an emphatic "yes!" Even if you do not agree with me right now, let yourself be open to the possibility of such development. Let us carry out some experiments together; perhaps we may then find some answers.

From my own limited experience, I am convinced that through constant training one can change one's mind: in other words, our positive attitudes, thoughts, and outlook can be enhanced, and their negative counterparts can be reduced. One of the main reasons is that the occurrence of even a single mental event depends on many factors; when these various factors are affected, the mind also changes. This is a simple truth about the nature of mind.

ের্জ

Let me now explain some of the other benefits of altruism and a good heart that may not be so obvious to us. As explained earlier, from the perspective of the vehicles of humans and divine beings, the ultimate purpose, or aim, of existence is to achieve a favorable birth in our next life, a goal that can only be attained by restraining from actions that are harmful to others. Therefore, even in the context of such an aim, we find that altruism and a good heart are at the root.

Moreover, the various features and aspects of human life, such as longevity, good health, success, happiness, and so forth, which we consider desirable, are all dependent on kindness and a good heart. These are basic qualities of human nature. It is also very clear that for a bodhisattva to be successful in accomplishing the practice of the *six perfections*—generosity, ethical discipline, tolerance, joyous effort, concentration, and wisdom—cooperation with and kindness towards fellow sentient beings are extremely important.

Thus, we find that kindness and a good heart form the underlying foundation for our success in this life, our progress on the spiritual path, and our fullfilment of our ultimate aspiration, the attainment of full enlightenment. Hence, kindness and a good heart are not only important at the beginning but also in the middle and at the end. Their necessity and value are not limited to any specific time, place, society, or culture.

Since compassion and a good heart are developed through constant and conscious effort, it is important for us first to identify the favorable conditions that give rise to our own qualities of kindness and a good heart, as well as the adverse circumstances that obstruct our cultivation of these positive states of mind. It is therefore important for us to lead a life of constant mindfulness and mental alertness. Our mastery of these faculties should be such that whenever a new situation arises, we are able to immediately recognize whether the circumstances are favorable or adverse to the development of compassion and a good heart. By pursuing the practice of compassion in such a manner, we will gradually be able to alleviate the effects of the obstructive forces and enhance the conditions that favor the development of compassion and a good heart.

10

RECOGNIZING THE ENEMY WITHIN

THE GREATEST OBSTACLE for cultivating compassion and a good
heart is selfishness: the attitude that cherishes one's own welfare and benefit, while often remaining oblivious to the well-
being of others. This self-centered attitude underlies most of our
ordinary states of mind, as well as the various states of existence
in samsara, and thus is the root of all delusions. Therefore, the
first task of a practitioner of compassion and a good heart is to
gain an understanding of the destructive nature of the delusions
and how they naturally lead to undesirable consequences.

To aid us in considering the destructive nature of the delusions and the undesirability of their effects, I will quote from the
Bodhicaryāvatāra. In the fourth chapter, entitled "Conscientiousness," Śāntideva explains that delusions such as hatred, anger,
attachment, and jealousy, which reside within our minds, are our
true enemies. As can be seen from the following two verses, he
states that these enemies do not have physical bodies with legs
and arms, nor do they hold weapons in their hands; instead,
they reside in our minds and afflict us from within. They control
us from within and bind us to them as their slaves. Normally,
however, we do not realize that these delusions are our enemies,
and so we never confront or challenge them. Since we do not
challenge the delusions, they reside unthreatened within our
mind and continue to inflict harm on us at will.

> The enemies such as hatred and craving
> Have neither arms nor legs,

And are neither courageous nor wise;
How, then, have I been used like a slave by them?

For while they dwell within my mind,
At their pleasure they cause me harm;
Yet I patiently endure them without anger.
But this is an inappropriate and shameful time for
  patience.[37]

Negative thoughts and emotions are often deceptive. They play tricks on us. Desire, for example, appears to us as a trusted friend, something beautiful and dear to us. Similarly, anger and hatred appear to us like our protectors or reliable body guards. Sometimes, when someone is about to harm you, anger rises up like a protector and gives you a kind of strength. Even though you may be physically weaker than your assailant, anger makes you feel strong. It gives you a false sense of power and energy, the result being, in this case, that you might get yourself beaten up. Because anger and other destructive emotions appear in such deceptive guises, we never actually challenge them. There are many similar ways in which the negative thoughts and emotions deceive us. In order to realize fully the treachery of these negative thoughts and emotions, we must first achieve a calm state of mind. Only then will we begin to see their treacherous nature.

If we look at human history, we will find that a good heart has been the key in achieving what the world regards as great accomplishments: for example, in the fields of civil rights, social work, political liberation, religion, and so forth. A sincere outlook and motivation do not belong exclusively to the sphere of religion; they can be generated by anyone simply by having genuine concern for others, for one's community, for the poor and the needy. In short, they arise from taking a deep interest in and being concerned about the welfare of the larger community, i.e., the welfare of others. Actions resulting from this kind of attitude and motivation will go down in history as good, beneficial, and a service to humanity. Today, when we read these things from history, although the events are in the past and have become only memories, we still feel happy and comforted because of them. We recall with a deep sense of admiration that this or that person did great and noble work. We can also see a few examples of such greatness in our own generation.

On the other hand, our history also abounds with stories of individuals perpetrating the most destructive and harmful acts: killing and torture, bringing misery and untold suffering to large numbers of people. These incidents in human history can be seen as reflecting the darker side of our common human heritage. These events occur only when there is hatred, anger, jealousy, and unbounded greed. World history is a record of the effects of the negative and positive thoughts of human beings. This, I think, is quite clear. By reflecting on these past occurrences, we can see that if we want to have a better and happier future, now is the time to examine the mindset of our present generation and to reflect on the way of life that it may bring about in the future. The pervasive power of these negative attitudes cannot be overstated.

Despite being a monk and a supposed practitioner of the *Bodhicaryāvatāra*, I myself still occasionally become irritated and angry and, as a result, use harsh words towards others. Then, a few moments later when the anger has subsided, I feel embarrassed; the negative words are already spoken, and there is truly no way to take them back. Although the words themselves are uttered and the sound of the voice has ceased to exist, their impact still lives on. Hence, the only thing I can do is to go to the person and apologize, isn't that right? But in the meantime, one feels quite shy and embarrassed. This shows that even a short instance of anger and irritation creates a great amount of discomfort and disturbance to the agent, not to mention the harm caused to the person who is the target of that anger. So in reality, these negative states of mind obscure our intelligence and judgment and, in this way, cause great damage.

One of the best human qualities is our intelligence, which enables us to judge what is wholesome and what is unwholesome, what is beneficial and what is harmful. Negative thoughts, such as anger and strong attachment, destroy this special human quality; this is indeed very sad. When anger or attachment dominates the mind, a person becomes almost crazed, and I am certain that nobody wishes to be crazy. Under their power we commit all kinds of acts—often having far-reaching and destructive consequences. A person gripped by such states of mind and emotion is like a blind person, who cannot see where he is going. Yet we neglect to challenge these negative thoughts and emotions, which lead to near insanity. On the contrary, we often nurture and reinforce them! By doing so we are, in fact, making ourselves prey to their destructive power. When you reflect along these lines, you will realize that our true enemy is not outside ourselves.

Let me give you another example. When your mind is trained in self-discipline, even if you are surrounded by hostile forces, your peace of mind will hardly be disturbed. On the other hand, your mental peace and calm can easily be disrupted by your own negative thoughts and emotions. So I repeat, the real enemy is within, not outside. Usually we define our enemy as a person, an external agent, whom we believe is causing harm to us or to someone we hold dear. But such an enemy is relative and impermanent. One moment, the person may act as an enemy; at yet another moment, he or she may become your best friend. This is a truth that we often experience in our own lives. But negative thoughts and emotions, the inner enemy, will always remain the enemy. They are your enemy today, they have been your enemy in the past, and they will remain your enemy in the future as long as they reside within your mental continuum. Therefore, Śāntideva says that negative thoughts and emotions are the real enemy, and this enemy is within.

This inner enemy is extremely dangerous. The destructive potential of an external enemy is limited, compared to that of its inner counterpart. Moreover, it is often possible to create a physical defense against an external enemy. In the past, for example, even though they had limited material resources and technological capabilities, people defended themselves by building fortresses and castles with many tiers and layers of walls. In today's nuclear age, such defenses as castles and fortresses are obsolete. In a time when every country is a potential target for the nuclear weapons of others, human beings still continue to develop defense systems of greater and greater sophistication. The strategic defense project initiated by the United States, widely known as "Star Wars," is a typical example of such a defense system. Underlying its development is still the old belief that we can eventually create a system that will provide us with the "ultimate" protection. I do not know if it will ever be possible to create a defense system capable of guaranteeing worldwide protection against all external forces of destruction. However, one thing is certain: as long as those destructive internal enemies are left to themselves, unchallenged, the threat of physical annihilation will always loom over us. In fact, the destructive power of an external enemy ultimately derives from the power of these internal forces. The inner enemy is the trigger that unleashes the destructive power of the external enemy.

The only effective means by which to overcome the inner enemy is through gaining a deep insight into and clearly realizing the nature of the mind. I always tell people that the mind is a very complex phenomenon. According to Buddhist philosophy, there are many types of mind, or consciousness. In scientific research, we analyze matter in terms of the particles that constitute its existence. We actualize the potential of the various molecular and chemical compositions and atomic structures that have beneficial value, while we neglect, or in some cases deliberately eliminate, those that lack such useful properties.

71

This discriminatory approach has certainly led to some interesting results. If the world paid a similar amount of attention to analyzing our inner world, the world of experience and mental phenomena, we would discover that there are multitudes of mental states, differing in their modes of apprehension, object, degree of intensity of engagement with their object, their phenomenological characteristics, and so on. Certain aspects of mind are useful and beneficial, so we should correctly identify them and enhance their potential. Like scientists, if we discover upon examination that certain states of mind are unwholesome in that they bring us suffering and problems, then we should realize the significance of this insight and seek a way to eradicate them. This is indeed a most worthwhile project. In fact, this should be your greatest concern in your practice of Dharma. It is quite similar to opening one's skull to carry out experiments on those tiny cells with the aim of determining which cells bring us joy and which cells cause disturbances. Śāntideva tells us that as long as these inner enemies remain secure within, there is great danger.

Śāntideva goes on to say that even if everyone in the world were to stand up against you as your enemies and harm you, as long as your own mind was disciplined and calm, they would not be able to disturb your peace. Yet a single instance of delusion arising in your mind has the power to disturb that peace and inner stability.

> Should even all the gods and anti-gods
> Rise up against me as my enemies,
> They could neither lead nor place me
> In the roaring fires of deepest hell.

> But the mighty foe, these disturbing conceptions,
> In a moment, can cast me amidst (those flames),
> Which when met will cause not even the ashes
> Of the king of mountains to remain.[38]

e/s⧢e/s

Śāntideva also states that one crucial difference between the ordinary enemy and the delusions is that if you relate in a friendly manner and with understanding towards the ordinary enemy, then you might be able to change that enemy into a friend, but you cannot relate to the delusions in a similar way. The more you try to associate with them with the aim of befriending them, the more harmful and disastrous they become.

> If I agreeably honor and entrust myself (to others),
> They will bring me benefit and happiness;
> But if I entrust myself to these disturbing conceptions,
> In the future they will bring only misery and harm.[39]

As I mentioned earlier, by training the mind and bringing about an inner discipline you can change your outlook and, thus, your behavior as well. Take my own case, for instance. People usually regard Tibetans who come from Amdo as short-tempered. So in Tibet, when someone would lose his or her temper, people would often take it as a sign that the person was from Amdo! This is the region that I come from. However, if I compare my temperament now to the way it was when I was between the ages of fifteen and twenty, I perceive a noticeable change. These days, I hardly find myself being irritated, and even when I am, it doesn't last long. This is a marvelous benefit—now I am always quite cheerful! It is, I think, the result of my own practice and training. In my lifetime, I have lost my country and have been reduced to being totally dependent on the goodwill of others. I have also lost my mother, and most of my tutors and gurus have passed away, although I now have a few new gurus. Of course, these are tragic incidents, and I feel sad when I think about them. However, I don't feel overwhelmed by sadness. Old, familiar faces disappear, and new faces appear, but I still maintain my happiness and peace of mind.

This capacity to relate to events from a broader perspective is, for me, one of the marvels of human nature.

As long as you remain under the domination of the delusions and their underlying states of ignorance, you have no possibility of achieving genuine, lasting happiness. This, I think, is a natural fact. If you feel deeply disturbed by this truth, you should respond by seeking a state of freedom from it—that is, the state of nirvana. Especially, if you are a monk or nun you should direct your life towards the attainment of nirvana, or true liberation. So if you can afford to devote yourself wholly to the practice of Dharma, then you should implement the spiritual methods in your life that lead to the attainment of this state of freedom. If, as in my own case, you do not have sufficient time, it is quite difficult, isn't it? I know that one factor preventing me from devoting myself fully to such a committed way of life is my own laziness. I am a rather lazy Dalai Lama, the lazy Tenzin Gyatso! All right! Even if you cannot lead a single-minded life of Dharma practice, it is very beneficial to reflect on these teachings as much as possible and make efforts to consider as transitory all adverse circumstances and disturbances. Like ripples in a pool, they occur and soon disappear. Insofar as our lives are karmically conditioned, they are characterized by endless cycles of problems, which arise and then subside. One problem appears and passes, and soon another one begins. They come and go in a ceaseless continuum. However, the continuum of our consciousness— for example, Tenzin Gyatso's consciousness—is beginningless. Though in a state of constant flux, an ever-changing, dynamic process, the basic nature of consciousness never changes. Such is the nature of our conditioned existence, and the realization of this truth makes it easy for me to relate to reality. This realistic outlook helps me maintain my peace and calm. This is Bhikṣu Tenzin Gyatso's way of thinking. Through my own experience, I know that the mind can be trained, and by means of that training, we can bring about a profound change within ourselves.

That much, I know, is quite certain.

Despite its pervasive influence and destructive potential, there is one particular way in which the inner enemy is weaker than the external enemy. Śāntideva explains in the *Bodhicaryāvatāra* that to overcome ordinary enemies you need physical strength and weapons. You might even need to spend billions of dollars on weapons to counter them. But to combat the enemy within, the disturbing conceptions, you need only develop the factors that give rise to the wisdom realizing the ultimate nature of phenomena. You do not need any material weapon nor do you need physical strength. This is very true.

> Deluded disturbing conceptions! When forsaken
>   by the wisdom eye
> And dispelled from my mind, where will you go?
> Where will you dwell in order to be able to injure me again?
> But, weak-minded, I have been reduced to making
>   no effort.[40]

Actually, when I was receiving the oral teachings on this text from the late Kunu Lama Rinpoche, I remarked that the *Bodhicaryāvatāra* states that delusions are humble and weak, which is not true. He immediately responded by saying that you do not need an atom bomb to destroy the delusions! So this is what Śāntideva means here. You do not need expensive sophisticated weapons to destroy the inner enemy. You simply need to develop a firm determination to defeat them by generating wisdom: a realization of the true nature of the mind. You must also genuinely understand both the relative nature of negative thoughts and emotions as well as the ultimate nature of all phenomena. In technical Buddhist terminology, this insight is known as the *true insight into the nature of emptiness.* Śāntideva mentions still another sense in which the inner enemy is weaker. Unlike an external enemy, the inner enemy cannot regroup and launch a comeback once it has been destroyed from within.

11

OVERCOMING ANGER AND HATRED

WE HAVE DISCUSSED THE DECEPTIVE and destructive nature of the delusions. Hatred and anger are the greatest obstacles for a practitioner of bodhicitta. Bodhisattvas should never generate hatred, but instead, they should counteract it. For this purpose, the practice of patience, or tolerance, is crucial. Śāntideva begins the sixth chapter of his text, entitled "Patience," by explaining the seriousness of the harm and damage caused by anger and hatred: they harm us now and in the future, and they also harm us by destroying our collection of past merits. Since the practitioner of patience must counteract and overcome hatred, Śāntideva emphasizes the importance of first identifying the factors that cause anger and hatred. The principal cause is dissatisfaction and unhappiness. When we are unhappy and dissatisfied, we easily become frustrated and this leads to feelings of hatred and anger.

Śāntideva explains that it is very important for those of us training in patience to prevent mental unhappiness from arising—as is prone to occur when you feel that you or your loved ones are threatened, or when misfortune befalls you, or when others obstruct your goals. Your feelings of dissatisfaction and unhappiness on these occasions are the fuel that feeds hatred and anger. So right from the beginning, it is important not to allow such circumstances to disturb your peace of mind.

He emphasizes that we should, with all the means at our disposal, counteract and eliminate the onset of hatred since its only function is to harm us and others. This is very profound advice.

Having found its fuel of dissatisfaction
In the prevention of what I wish for
And in the doing of what I do not want,
Hatred increases and then destroys me.[41]

If maintaining a balanced and happy state of mind even in the face of adversity is a key factor in preventing hatred from arising, we still may wonder how to achieve it. Śāntideva says that when you are faced with adverse circumstances, feeling unhappy serves no purpose in overcoming the undesirable situation. It is not only futile but will, in fact, only serve to aggravate your own anxiety and bring about an uncomfortable and dissatisfied state of mind. You lose all sense of composure and happiness. Anxiety and unhappiness gradually eat away inside you and affect your sleep patterns, your appetite, and your health as well. In fact, if the initial harm you experienced was inflicted by an enemy, your mental unhappiness may even become a source of delight for that person. Therefore, it is pointless to feel unhappy and dissatisfied when faced with adverse circumstances or, for that matter, to retaliate against the agent who caused you harm.

Śāntideva further reasons that if the problem can be resolved, there is no need to be overly concerned or disturbed. On the other hand, if nothing can be done to resolve the difficulty, it is useless to feel unhappy about it. Either way, being unhappy and overwhelmed by the difficulty is not an appropriate response.

Generally, there are two types of hatred or anger that result from unhappiness and dissatisfaction. One type is when someone inflicts harm upon you, and as a result, you feel unhappy and generate anger. Another type is when, although no person may be directly inflicting harm upon you, as a result of seeing the success and prosperity of your enemies, you feel unhappy and generate anger on that basis.

Similarly, there are generally two types of harm caused by others. One type is direct physical harm inflicted by others and consciously experienced by you. The other type is harm done to your material possessions, reputation, friendship, and so on. Though not directed at your body, these acts are also a type of harm. Let us say that a person hits you with a stick, and you feel pain and become angry. You don't feel angry towards the very instrument of the pain, that is, the stick, do you? What exactly is the object of your anger? If it would be appropriate to feel angry toward the factor that impelled the act of hitting, then you should not be angry with the person but with the negative emotions that compelled that person to act. Ordinarily, however, we do not make such distinctions. Instead, we consider the person—the intermediary agent between the negative emotions and the act—as solely responsible, and we hold a grudge against him—not against the stick, nor against the delusions.

We should also be aware that since we possess a physical body that is susceptible to pain when hit by a stick, our own body partly contributes to our experience of pain. Because of our body and its nature, we experience physical pain even when no external causes of pain are present. It is clear then that the experience of pain or suffering comes about as a result of interaction between both our own body and various external factors.

You can also reflect on how, if inflicting harm on others is the essential nature of the person who is harming you, there is no point in being angry since there would be nothing that you or that person could do to change his or her essential nature. If it were truly the person's nature to inflict harm, the person would simply be unable to act otherwise. As stated by Śāntideva:

> Even if it were the nature of the childish
> To cause harm to other beings,
> It would still be incorrect to be angry with them.
> For this would be like begrudging fire for having the
> nature to burn.[42]

On the other hand, if harming is not the person's essential nature but, instead, their apparently harmful character is merely incidental and circumstantial, then there is still no need to feel angry towards that person since the problem is entirely due to certain immediate conditions and circumstances. For example, he may have lost his temper and acted badly, even though he did not really mean to hurt you. It is possible to think along these lines as well.

When you feel angry towards others who are not causing you direct, physical harm but whom you perceive as getting in the way of your acquisition of fame, position, material gains, and so forth, you should think in the following manner: Why should I get especially upset or angry about this particular problem? Analyze the nature of what you are being kept from obtaining— fame and so on—and examine carefully their benefit to you. Are they really that important? You will find that they are not. Since that is the case, why be so angry towards that person? Thinking in this way is also useful.

When you become angry as a result of the unhappiness you feel at seeing your enemies' success and prosperity, you should remember that simply being hateful, angry, or unhappy is not going to affect that person's material possessions or their success in life. Therefore, even from that point of view, it is quite pointless.

In addition to the practice of patience, those practitioners who take Śāntideva's text as inspiration are also seeking to develop bodhicitta—the altruistic attitude to achieve enlightenment for the benefit of all sentient beings—as well as compassion and thought transformation. If, despite their practice, they still feel unhappy about their enemies' success in life, then they should remember that this attitude is very inappropriate for a practitioner of bodhicitta. If this negative attitude persists, the thought "I am a practitioner of bodhicitta; I am someone who lives according to the precepts of thought transformation" becomes mere words devoid of meaning. Instead, a true practitioner of bodhicitta should rejoice that others have been able to achieve something on their own without one's help. Rather than being unhappy and hateful, we should rejoice in the success of others.

If we investigate on a still deeper level, we will find that when enemies inflict harm on us, we can actually feel gratitude towards them. Such situations provide us with a rare opportunity to put to test our own practice of patience. It is a precious occasion to practice not only patience but the other bodhisattva ideals as well. As a result, we have the opportunity to accumulate merit in these situations and to receive the benefits thereof. The poor enemy, on the other hand, because of the negative action of inflicting harm on someone out of anger and hatred, must eventually face the consequences of his or her own actions. It is almost as if the perpetrator of the harm sacrifices himself or herself for the sake of our benefit. Since the merit accumulated from the practice of patience was possible only because of the opportunity provided us by our enemy, strictly speaking, we should dedicate our merit to the benefit of that enemy. This is why the *Bodhicaryāvatāra* speaks of the kindness of the enemy.

Although we might recognize, on the one hand, the kindness of the enemy, we might feel, on the other, that the enemy had no intention to be kind to us. Therefore, we think, it is not necessary for us to remember his kindness at all. If, in order to respect or hold something dear, there must be conscious intent from the side of the object, then this argument should apply equally to other subjects as well. For example, from their sides, the true cessation of suffering and the true paths leading to cessation have no conscious intention to be beneficial. Yet, we still respect and revere them. Why? Because we derive benefit from them. If the benefits we derive justify our reverence and respect for these two Noble Truths, despite their not having any conscious intention, then this same rationale should apply to the enemy as well.

However, you might feel that there is a major difference between the enemy and the two Truths: true cessation and true paths. Unlike the two Truths, the enemy has a conscious will to harm you. But this difference is also not a valid reason not to respect the enemy. In fact, if anything, it is additional grounds to revere and be grateful to your enemy. It is indeed this special factor that makes your enemy unique. If the mere inflicting of physical pain were sufficient to make someone an enemy, you would have to consider your doctor an enemy, for he often causes pain during treatment. Now, as a genuine practitioner of compassion and bodhicitta, you must develop tolerance. And in order to practice sincerely and to develop patience, you need someone who willfully hurts you. Thus, these people give us real opportunities to practice these things. They are testing our inner strength in a way that even our guru cannot. Even the Buddha possesses no such potential. Therefore, the enemy is *the only one* who gives us this golden opportunity. That is a remarkable conclusion, isn't it! By thinking along these lines and using these reasons, you will eventually develop a kind of extraordinary respect towards your enemies. This is Śāntideva's primary message in the sixth chapter.

Once you generate genuine respect towards your enemy, you can then easily remove most of the major obstacles to developing infinite altruism. Śāntideva mentions in the *Bodhicaryāvatāra* that, just as the field of buddhas contributes greatly to one's achievement of omniscience, there is an equal contribution from sentient beings as well. Omniscience can only be achieved in reliance upon both of these fields: the kindness of sentient beings, and the kindness of the buddhas.

For those of us who claim to be followers of Buddha Śākyamuni and who revere and respect the bodhisattva ideals, Śāntideva states that it is incorrect to hold grudges or have hatred towards our enemies, when all the buddhas and bodhisattvas hold all sentient beings dear to their hearts. Of course, our enemies are included within the field of all sentient beings. If we hold grudges towards those whom the buddhas and bodhisattvas hold close to their hearts, we contradict the ideals and experience of the buddhas and bodhisattvas, those very beings whom we are trying to emulate.

Even in worldly terms, the more respect and affection we feel towards any person, the more consideration we have for them. We try to avoid acting in ways that they might disapprove of, thinking that we might offend them. We try to take into consideration our friend's way of thinking, their principles, and so on. If we do this even for our ordinary friends, then, as practitioners of the bodhisattva ideals, we should show the same, if not higher, regard for the buddhas and bodhisattvas, by trying not to hold grudges and hateful feelings towards our enemies.

Śāntideva concludes this chapter on patience by explaining the benefits of practicing patience. In summary, through practicing patience, not only will you reach a state of omniscience in the future, but even in your everyday life, you will experience its practical benefits. You will be able to maintain your peace of mind and live a joyful life.

When we practice patience to overcome hatred and anger, it is important to be equipped with the force of joyous effort. We should be skillful in cultivating joyous effort. Śāntideva explains that, just as we must be mindful when undertaking an ordinary task, such as waging war, to inflict the greatest possible destruction on the enemy while at the same time protecting ourselves from the enemy's harm, in the same way, when we undertake the practice of joyous effort, it is important to attain the greatest level of success while assuring that this action does not damage or hinder our other practices.

12

ONESELF AND OTHERS:
EXCHANGING PLACES

IN THE CHAPTER ON MEDITATION in the *Bodhicaryāvatāra*, we find an explanation of the actual meditation for cultivating bodhicitta, the aspiration to achieve enlightenment for the benefit of all living beings. Śāntideva bases his instructions on Nāgārjuna's *Ratnāvali (Precious Garland)*.[43] Therefore, the techniques for cultivating this altruistic aspiration are explained according to the method of equalizing and exchanging oneself and others.[44]

Equalizing oneself and others means to develop the attitude and understanding of, "Just as I desire happiness and wish to avoid suffering, the same is true of all other living beings, who are infinite as space; they too desire happiness and wish to avoid suffering." Śāntideva explains that, just as we work for our own benefit in order to gain happiness and protect ourselves from suffering, we should also work for the benefit of others, to help them attain happiness and freedom from suffering.

Śāntideva argues that, although there are different parts to our body, such as our head, limbs, and so on, insofar as the need to protect them is concerned, there is no difference amongst them, for they are all equally parts of the same body. In the same manner, all sentient beings have this natural tendency—wishing to attain happiness and be free from suffering—and, insofar as that natural inclination is concerned, there is no difference whatsoever between all sentient beings. Consequently, we should not discriminate between ourselves and others in working to gain happiness and overcome suffering.

We should reflect upon and make serious efforts to dissolve our attitude that views ourselves and others as being separate and distinct. We have seen that insofar as the wish to gain happiness and to avoid suffering is concerned, there is no difference at all. The same is also true of our *natural right* to be happy; just as we have the right to enjoy happiness and freedom from suffering, all other living beings have the same natural right. So wherein lies the difference? The difference lies in the number of sentient beings involved. When we speak of the welfare of ourselves, we are speaking of the welfare of only one individual, whereas the welfare of others encompasses the well-being of an infinite number of beings. From that point of view, we can understand that others' welfare is much more important than our own.

If our own and others' welfare were totally unrelated and independent of one another, we could make a case for neglecting others' welfare. But that is not the case. I am always related to others and heavily dependent on them: while I am an ordinary person, while I am on the path, and also once I have achieved the resultant state. If we reflect along these lines, the importance of working for the benefit of others emerges naturally.

You should also examine whether, by remaining selfish and self-centered despite the validity of the above points, you can still achieve happiness and fulfill your desires. If that were the case, then pursuit of your selfish and self-centered habits would be a reasonable course of action. But it is not. The nature of our existence is such that we must depend on the cooperation and kindness of others for our survival. It is an observable fact that the more we take the welfare of others to heart and work for their benefit, the more benefit we attain for ourselves. You can see this fact for yourself. On the other hand, the more selfish and self-centered you remain, the more lonely and miserable you become. You can also observe this fact yourself.

Therefore, if you definitely want to work for your own benefit and welfare, then, as the *Bodhicaryāvatāra* recommends, it is better to take into account the welfare of others and to regard their welfare as more important than your own. By contemplating these points, you will certainly be able to strengthen more and more your attitude of cherishing the well-being of others.

Furthermore, we can complement our practice of bodhicitta with meditations on the various factors of wisdom. For example, we can reflect upon buddha-nature: the potential to actualize buddhahood that resides within ourselves and all sentient beings. We can also reflect on the ultimate nature of phenomena, their empty nature, by using logical reasoning to ascertain the nature of reality. We can reflect that the cessation of suffering is possible because the ignorance that is its root cause is adventitious in nature and, hence, can be separated from the essential nature of our mind. By thinking and meditating on the factors of wisdom and maintaining a sustained practice of compassion and altruism with concerted effort over a long period of time, you will see a real change in your mind. This is why in the *Bodhicaryāvatāra*, we find that the discussion on the practice of bodhicitta is immediately followed by the chapter on wisdom. The wisdom chapter, unlike its preceding counterparts, is difficult and complex. I am confident that Śāntideva, who had great compassion and an admirable gift for expressing ideas simply and succinctly, would have done so if it were possible. But in the case of the wisdom chapter, he has not. So we must apply more effort and hard work from our side to understand this chapter satisfactorily. We must work harder; this is the only way.

13

QUESTIONS AND ANSWERS

Q: IN THE WEST, I find there is much pressure to do more and go fast. This leads to stress and impatience. Since Your Holiness has said it is best for Westerners not to leave the West, what specific methods or techniques does Your Holiness recommend for these stresses and impatience?

HHDL: That is difficult to say. It would depend a great deal on the mental attitude that you adopt. Although physically you may be very busy and in haste all the time, if you are able to maintain a calmness of mind, this might help. You might be better able to choose the best antidote by checking your own experience yourself.

Q: Your Holiness, given that politics is the number one system that affects the family, is it not essential that the people who truly live the bodhisattva way become active within politics or, at the least, objectively educate themselves?

HHDL: A *bodhisattva* is a person who cultivates the aspiration to achieve complete enlightenment for the benefit of all living beings and who has also pledged to engage in the deeds that are the most beneficial in fulfilling this aim of working for others. This may include the field of politics. If a bodhisattva feels with some certainty that by taking an active part in politics he or she can bring about a great change within the community or society, then that bodhisattva should definitely engage in politics.

Q: Your Holiness, yesterday you treated the relationship we should have with our enemy. What do Buddhist scriptures say about the mentally ill?

HHDL: Buddhist scriptures speak of being exceptionally kind and compassionate to these people. One of the most important ideals of the bodhisattva practices is to be especially compassionate towards those who most need help, such as those with physical and mental disabilities.

PART III

THE VAJRAYANA BUDDHISM OF TIBET

14

THE DISTINCTIVE FEATURES OF TANTRA

Now I will talk a little about Buddhist tantra, the system of thought and practice known as Vajrayana.

There are some chronological issues concerning the evolution of the teachings of Buddhist tantra, questions of when and where the Buddha taught the various tantras.[45] However, we need not presume that all of the teachings of tantra were propounded by the Buddha during his historical lifetime. Rather, I think that the teachings of tantra could have also emerged through the extraordinary insights of highly realized individuals who were able to explore to the fullest extent the physical elements and the potential within the human body and mind. As a result of such investigation, a practitioner can attain very high realizations and visions, thus enabling him or her to receive tantric teachings at a mystical level. Therefore, when we reflect on tantric teachings, we should not limit our perspective by rigid notions of time and space.

Although it seems that there are a few sets of tantras belonging to the lower classes of tantra that the Buddha himself taught while in his ordinary form as a fully ordained monk, in most cases he taught each tantra after having assumed the form of the principal deity of the mandala of that particular tantra.

The practice of tantra can be undertaken when a person has a firm foundation in the essential features of the path to enlightenment as explained in the sutra system, that is, the teachings of the Buddhist sutras explained previously. This means that you should have an attitude that wishes to abandon completely the causes of suffering, a correct view of emptiness as taught in the second turning of the wheel, and some realization of bodhi-citta—the altruistic aspiration, based on love and compassion, to achieve enlightenment for the benefit of all living beings. Your understanding of these, together with your practice of the six perfections, enable you to lay a proper foundation of the path common to sutra and tantra. Only then can you properly under-take a successful practice of tantra.

The profundity of tantra emerges in its fullest extent in the teachings and the practice of Highest Yoga Tantra. For example, the full meaning of expressions such as "stainless wisdom," "the essence of buddhahood," and so forth, which we find in certain scriptures belonging to the third turning of the wheel, emerges only in Highest Yoga Tantra. Regardless of whether or not we maintain that the *Uttaratantra* speaks explicitly about the funda-mental innate mind of clear light, it is this fundamental nature of mind that is the ultimate meaning of the essence of buddha-hood, or buddha-nature. Thus, the ultimate intent of that teaching on buddha-nature should be understood in terms of the fundamental innate mind of clear light, which is taught explicitly and extensively in Highest Yoga Tantra.

Highest Yoga Tantra is considered to be unique and most pro-found in its approach. It not only explains and outlines the methods for realizing the path at the gross level of mind, but it also teaches various techniques and methods for utilizing the subtle levels of mind—especially the fundamental innate mind of clear light—transforming them into the entity of the path to enlightenment. When you are able to transform the fundamental innate mind of clear light into the entity of the path, you are equipped with a very powerful practice.

Normally, when we undertake single-pointed meditation, we do so with the gross levels of our mind. Consequently, we require strong forces of mindfulness and alertness to maintain our focus on the object of meditation and prevent our mind from being swayed by distractions. Therefore, we must always be vigilant and conscious. Yet, if we could do away with the gross levels of mind—such as the conscious thought processes, which are very distracting—there would be no need for strong and constant vigilance and alertness. Thus, in Highest Yoga Tantra, a special meditative technique is explained by which we are able to dissolve and withdraw the gross levels of mind; we bring the mind to its subtlest level where there is no possibility of distractions arising.

From the perspective of general practice in Highest Yoga Tantra, the method of transforming the fundamental innate mind of clear light—that is, the subtlest level of mind—into the entity of the path is to dissolve and withdraw both the gross levels of mind and the wind-energies that propel these gross minds. The three main ways of doing this are (1) through the yoga of wind, or *prāṇayoga*, (2) through generating the experiences of the four types of bliss, and (3) through cultivating the state of non-conceptuality.[46]

It is important to be aware that not only are there these diverse methods, but also that they are quite distinct from each other. We can achieve the feat of dissolving and withdrawing the gross minds and the corresponding energies using any of these three different techniques. We should, however, make a distinction here. Although one can achieve this feat by means of any one of the methods mentioned earlier, this does not mean that one method alone will suffice. The practice of the main technique must be complemented by various other factors. For example, if we generate a virtuous thought today, this virtuous thought can then serve as a cause for attaining omniscience in the future. This, however, does not mean that the virtuous thought we generated is the sole cause of the resulting omniscience.

In *Mañjuśrīmukhāgama* (*Sacred Words of Mañjuśrī*), a text on the Completion Stage of Guhyasamāja Mañjuśrīvajra,[47] the Indian master Buddhaśrījñāna states that because of the physical structure of our human bodies on this planet and the elements that we possess, even on the ordinary level there are certain occasions during which we naturally have slight experiences of the subtle level of mind called clear light or the non-conceptual state. These occasions are during sleep, sneezing, fainting, and sexual climax. This shows that we have within ourselves a certain potential or seed, which can be developed further. Among these four naturally occurring states, the one that accords us the best opportunity to generate the experience of clear light is during sexual climax. Although we are using this ordinary term "sexual," the reference should not be taken in the ordinary way. The reference here is to the experience of entering into union with a consort of the opposite sex, through which the vital elements located at the crown are melted, and then, through the power of meditation, their flow is reversed upward. One of the prerequisites for engaging in such an advanced practice of sexual union is that the practitioner should have the ability to abstain from the fault of emission. Emission of sexual fluids is said to be damaging to one's practice, particularly according to the explanations found in the *Kālacakra Tantra*. This tantra emphasizes that a tantric practitioner should be able to protect himself or herself from emission even while dreaming. Hence, the tantras describe various techniques enabling the meditator to prevent emission in dreams. This is in contrast to the monastic rules of the Vinaya wherein the Buddha made exception for the experience of emission during dream states. In the Vinaya context, such emission is considered to be beyond the practitioner's conscious control whereas in tantra it is specifically emphazied that one should try to protect from emission even during dream states.

In order for the experience of actually melting the *bodhicitta*[48] to take place, we, as meditators, must generate the feelings of desire we normally experience in relation to a sexually attractive person. By virtue of the force of that desire, you are able to melt the elements within your body, resulting in the experience of a non-conceptual state. At that point, you should direct your attention toward, and focus on, the mind of enlightenment.

As a result of the bodhicitta melting within one's body, the experience of a blissful non-conceptual state arises. If you are able to generate that blissful state into the experience of emptiness, then you have achieved the feat of transforming a delusion into the wisdom realizing emptiness, since this wisdom was formerly an afflictive emotion, namely, desire. When you are able to utilize that non-conceptual state—that is, the blissful mind—to realize emptiness, the wisdom thus generated becomes exceptionally powerful and serves as the antidote that counteracts all afflictive emotional and cognitive states. Therefore, in one sense, we can say it is delusion itself—in the form of the wisdom derived from delusion—that actually destroys the delusions, for it is the blissful experience of emptiness induced by sexual desire that dissolves the force of sexual impulses. This is analogous to the life of wood-born insects: they consume the very wood from which they are born. Such utilization of the delusions, as an intregral part of the path to enlightenment, is a unique feature of tantra.

To illustrate this point, when the Buddha taught the various higher tantras, he did so while appearing as the principal deity of the respective mandala in union with consort. Therefore, practitioners must also, in their imaginations, visualize themselves in the divine aspect of a deity in union with consort.

Another unique feature of tantra concerns the process of attaining the two *kāyas*, or embodiments of an enlightened being, the Form Body, or *rūpakāya*, and the Truth Body, or *dharmakāya*. According to the sutra system, by cultivating the altruistic aspiration to achieve the completely enlightened state, the practitioner also aspires to attain the two enlightened embodiments. However, this dual body of an enlightened being does not arise without causes and conditions—specifically, causes and conditions that are concordant. This means that causes and their effects must possess significantly similar features. Given this, the sutra system speaks of the causes of the enlightened Form Body in terms of the unique mental body achieved only by bodhisattvas on the highest levels. This serves as the substantial cause that, through progressive stages of purification, eventually leads to the actualization of the Form Body of an enlightened being. The scriptures of the Individual Vehicle emphasize this point as well. Although the Individual Vehicle teachings do not expound complete methods and causes for actualizing the omniscient state, they do speak of certain practices directed toward achieving the various major and minor marks of an enlightened being, a buddha.

Tantra has a unique method for attaining the enlightened Form Body, and in Highest Yoga Tantra, not only are these unique causes and methods for actualizing the Form Body outlined, but those for attaining the enlightened Truth Body are explained as well. Before undertaking the meditative practice that serves as the substantial and principal cause of the enlightened Form Body (and is, therefore, the method for attaining it), practitioners of tantra should first ripen their mental faculties. In other words, one should "rehearse" for the attainment of such a unique cause. This is the principal significance of *deity yoga*—where the meditator visualizes himself or herself in the form of a deity.

Explanatory tantras, such as the *Vajra-Tent Tantra* (*Vajrapañjaratantra*), and related Indian commentaries point out that the attainment of the enlightened Truth Body requires meditation and practice of a path with features similar to the resultant state. The practice of meditation on emptiness through direct intuition, where all dualistic appearances and the elaborations of conceptuality are withdrawn, is such a method. In the same manner, in order to obtain the enlightened Form Body, one must also cultivate a path possessing similar features to the resultant state: the Form Body of an enlightened being.

Engaging in a path with similar features to the resultant state of buddhahood—especially the Form Body—has great significance and power. It is also indispensable. Tantra speaks of the path being similar to the fruit in four ways. These are technically known as the four complete purities: (1) the complete purity of environment; (2) the complete purity of body; (3) the complete purity of resources; and (4) the complete purity of activities.

In order to achieve the resultant state, that is, the union of the two enlightened bodies, it is essential to engage in a path characterized by the union of method and wisdom. This fact is accepted by all Mahayana schools. However, the union of wisdom and method as explained in the sutra system is not complete. In the context of sutra, wisdom refers to the wisdom realizing emptiness, and method refers to the practice of the six perfections. The union of the two, therefore, is understood only in terms of the conjunction of two distinct factors that complement each other—that is to say, the wisdom realizing emptiness is complemented by the method aspects of the path, such as the practice of bodhicitta, compassion, and so forth. Similarly, the practice of bodhicitta and its related method aspects are complemented and supported by the wisdom factor—the realization of emptiness. In other words, in the sutra system, it is not possible to have both factors of the path—wisdom and method—complete within a single entity of consciousness.

Although it is true that when practicing the union of wisdom and method in the sutra system, wisdom is not isolated from method, and method is not isolated from wisdom; still, there is no full merging of the two. Therefore, sutra practice cannot serve as the ultimate cause, or path, of actualizing the resultant state of buddhahood, in which there is a complete unity of the two enlightened bodies: Form Body and Truth Body.

The question then follows, What form of practice, or path, combines method and wisdom in an inseparable unity? The answer is the tantric practice of deity yoga. In deity yoga, a single moment of consciousness apprehends the divine form of a deity while, at the same time, being clearly aware of its empty nature. So in this case, both meditation on the deity and an apprehension of emptiness coexist in complete form within a single cognitive moment. Such a moment of consciousness, therefore, contains both of the two factors of method and wisdom. It is known as "the Vajrasattva yoga of the indivisible union of method and wisdom."

Among the principal features of deity yoga meditation is the cultivation of the "pride," or self-identity, of a divine being in order to overcome our feelings and perception of ordinariness. I think this helps us to elicit to an even greater extent the potential for enlightenment from within us. Successful development of a firm identity as a deity requires a strong, stable visualization of the deity's form, or appearance. Normally, because of our natural tendencies and our sense of self, our innate feelings of "I" and "self" are based upon the composite of our ordinary body and mind. If we can successfully cultivate a clear and firm perception of ourselves in the divine aspect of the deity, we shall also be able to develop divine pride, a sense of exalted identity, based on that divine appearance.

In addition, in order to actualize omniscient mind within ourselves, we must possess the substantial causes that will eventually become omniscient mind. These substantial causes must be of the nature of consciousness—and not just any consciousness, but a consciousness with a very enduring continuity, and no other.

Let me summarize briefly. In order to actualize the omniscient mind of buddhahood, it is necessary to realize the nature of mind. This mind, whose nature we realize in order to actualize omniscience, must be a very special type of mind, which, in terms of its continuity, is eternal. It cannot be any other type of mind. Because the various contaminated states of mind, such as delusions and afflictive emotional and cognitive states, are adventitious, they are occasional: they arise in a certain moment but soon disappear. From that standpoint, they are not enduring. The mind whose nature we realize when we become omniscient should be eternal in terms of its continuity; it should not be adventitious. This signifies that one should be able to realize the

100

empty nature of a pure mind, that is, a mind whose essential nature has never been polluted by delusions.

When viewed from the perspective of emptiness itself, there is no difference between the emptiness of a mundane external phenomenon, such as a sprout, and the emptiness of a deity, such as Vairocana. But when viewed from the perspective of the object of emptiness, there is a vast difference. It is the wisdom that realizes this special type of emptiness, the emptiness of the deity, that eventually serves as the substantial cause for the omniscient mind of buddhahood. This, in brief, is the essence of deity yoga. Deity yoga encompasses the union of *clarity*—the visualization of the deity—and the *profound*—the realization of emptiness.

Also, according to the sutra system, with regard to the welfare and realizations of the path of non-Mahayana practitioners, the Buddha never made exceptions with regard to generating the delusions. For a bodhisattva, however, there are occasions mentioned in the sutras in which such exceptions are made if the application of certain types of delusion can be beneficial for the purposes of others. The Buddha has said in the Mahayana sutras that just as a town's manure, though it is dirty, is helpful as fertilizer on a farm, in the same manner the delusions of bodhisattvas can be beneficial for the well-being of others. Even so, within the context of sutra, he never made exceptions allowing for a bodhisattva to generate anger or hatred. Yet for ordinary people like us, anger is a strong, forceful emotion that sometimes actually seems to help expedite certain tasks. Therefore, we can understand why, in tantra, the Buddha also made exceptions allowing for the generation of anger—because in tantra, one finds techniques and methods for utilizing the emotional energy of anger, and even hatred, for positive purposes. Here, however, we must be aware that in order to utilize hatred and anger for positive purposes, we must continually maintain our original motivation: the altruistic aspiration to achieve enlightenment for the benefit of others. Induced by this primary, overriding intention, our actions may find their circumstantial impetus in anger or hatred. If this crucial point is appreciated, one can also understand the significance of the wrathful aspects of the deities in tantra.

Thus, in all the above ways that we have discussed in which practice of tantra is differentiated from practice in the sutra system, we can say that these are the distinctive features of the tantric path that render it superior.

15

THE DIVISIONS OF TANTRA

AS EXPLAINED IN THE *Vajra-Tent Tantra*, there are four classes within the tantric system. However, it is only in Highest Yoga Tantra that the profound and unique features of tantra find their fullest expression. Consequently, we should view the lower tantras as steps leading towards Highest Yoga Tantra. Although the presence of various methods of taking desire into the path is a feature common to all four classes of tantra, the level of desire employed differs considerably from one class of tantra to another. In the first class of tantra, one takes into the path the desire generated from merely gazing at an attractive person of the opposite sex. Then, the three remaining classes, respectively, employ the desire generated from smiling at and laughing with such a person, the desire involved in touching and holding hands, and finally, the desire involved in sexual union.

These four classes of tantra are named according to their functions as well as their different features. In the first, Action Tantra, the external actions of cleanliness, cleansing, and so forth, as well as of *mudrā*, or symbolic hand gestures, are emphasized as being more important than the inner yoga. Therefore, it is called *Action* Tantra. In the second class of tantra, Performance Tantra, there is an equal emphasis on both the inner and outer aspects. In the third class, Yoga Tantra, the inner yoga of meditative stabilization is emphasized more than external activities. The fourth class, Highest Yoga Tantra, is so called not only because it emphasizes the importance of inner yoga, but also because there is no class of tantra superior to it.

According to the explanations and particular terminology of the Nyingma school—specifically, the Great Perfection school, or *Dzog-chen*—we find references to a ninefold division of yānas, or Nine Graded Vehicles.[49] The first three are the Hearers', Solitary Realizers', and Bodhisattva Vehicles, referring to the three vehicles taught in the sutra system. They are also called the *three vehicles from the direction of the origin of suffering.* The second three are Action Tantra, Performance Tantra, and Yoga Tantra. These three are called the external vehicles or external tantras because of their emphasis on external activities, such as rituals, cleansing, and so forth. They are also referred to as *tantras of austere awareness,* because these tantric teachings advocate certain physical penances, such as fasting, maintaining special diets, and so on. Then there are the three inner tantras: Father Tantra, Mother Tantra, and Non-Dual Tantra, or in the terminology of the Great Perfection school, Mahāyoga, Anuyoga, and Mahātiyoga. These three inner vehicles are termed the *vehicles of overpowering means* because they contain methods for manifesting the subtlest level of mind by dissolving the gross levels of mind and energies, by which the practitioner brings his mental state to a deep level beyond the polarities of discriminating between good and bad, dirty or clean, and so on, and is thus able to transcend the worldly conventions governed by such polarities.

16

INITIATION: EMPOWERMENT

WITHIN THE FOUR CLASSES of tantra there are many subdivisions. Highest Yoga Tantra consists of certain categories, such as Father Tantra, Mother Tantra, and, in addition, according to some scholars, Non-Dual Tantra. Great scholars such as Taktsang Lotsawa Sherab Rinchen divide Highest Yoga Tantra into these three categories on the basis of the three initiations that ripen the various faculties of the trainee towards the realization of the Completion Stage. From this point of view, tantras emphasizing the secret initiation are categorized as Father Tantras, those emphasizing the wisdom-knowledge initiation, as Mother Tantras, and those emphasizing the fourth initiation, as Non-Dual Tantras. This manner of defining the three divisions within Highest Yoga Tantra has profound significance.

Just as the realization of bodhicitta—the aspiration to attain complete enlightenment for the sake of all living beings—is the entrance to the practice of the Bodhisattva Vehicle in the sutra system, in the same manner, receiving an empowerment, or initiation, is the only entrance to the practice of tantra. The general format of an empowerment ceremony is quite uniform among the three lower tantras. But in Highest Yoga Tantra, because there is great diversity among the tantras belonging to this category, there are also many different kinds of initiations, which serve as the ripening factors specific to those various tantras.

There are also differences in the number of empowerments necessary for each specific class of tantra. For example, in the case of Action Tantra, two are indispensable: the water empowerment and the crown empowerment. For Performance Tantra, the five wisdom initiations are indispensable. For Yoga Tantra, in addition to the five wisdom initiations, the vajra master empowerment is necessary. And in the case of Highest Yoga Tantra, all four empowerments—vase, secret, wisdom-knowledge, and word—are necessary.

You should be aware, however, that there are different terms used in the various traditions for these various empowerments. For example, in the Nyingma school, according to the Mahāyoga tradition, the vajra master initiation is called the *potential initiation*, and the vajra disciple initiation, the *beneficial initiation*. Another initiation, called the *all-encompassing* (or *condensed*) *vajra initiation*, is also mentioned. Moreover, in the Great Perfection school, the fourth initiation has four subdivisions—the initiations with elaboration, without elaboration, greatly free of elaboration, and perfectly free of elaboration.

Generally speaking, the original Sanskrit term *abhiṣeka*, often translated as initiation, or empowerment, has many different connotations. In its broadest sense, initiation is explained in various contexts: in terms of the ripening factor—the *causal initiation*; in terms of the *path initiation*—the path of release; and in terms of the purified result—the *initiation of the resultant state*. According to the Great Perfection school, there is one more type of initiation, the *initiation of the base*. *Base* here refers to the fundamental innate mind of clear light that serves as the basis and allows for the possibility of receiving all the other initiations. If we were lacking the basic faculty—the fundamental innate mind of clear light—there would be no possibility for any of the ensuing empowerments. For example, we cannot speak about the ripening factor—the path—and the resultant state on the basis of just any external phenomenon, such as a vase or a sprout. It is only on the basis of the individual possessing this inner faculty that we can speak of the ripening factor, the path leading to the resultant state, and so forth. Thus, broadly speaking, there are four types of initiation.

When we conduct an empowerment ceremony, a mandala is required. This is the celestial mansion, the pure residence of the deity. There are different types of mandalas: the mandala of concentration, the cloth-painted mandala, and the mandala of colored sand. Also, in Highest Yoga Tantra, there is the body mandala of the guru. There are also the conventional bodhicitta mandala, the ultimate bodhicitta mandala, and so on.

Among all these different kinds of mandalas, the colored sand mandala is the chief one.[50] Only in the preparation of this mandala can all the rituals of consecrating the site and the strings used for measurement be conducted, and it allows the possibility of performing the ritual dances involving different hand and leg postures. There are different types of ritual dance. One kind consists of different postures that are adopted when consecrating the site where the mandala will be built; another is performed at the end of having completed the mandala, as an offering to the mandala deities; yet another, popularly known as the Ceremonial Masked Dance, is mostly associated with rituals of overcoming interferences. Many small Tibetan monasteries are expert in performing these different rituals, but one can question the accuracy of their knowledge of the symbolism and significance behind the movements. Also, people generally seem to think of ceremonial masked dances as entertainment, a spectacle. This is, in fact, a sad and unfortunate sign of the degeneration of tantra.

I once read in an Indian history that one of the factors that caused the degeneration of Buddhist tantra in India was the proliferation of tantric practices that occurred during a certain period in the past. In fact, if a tantric practice lacks the basic foundation and prerequisites, then the techniques and meditations of tantra can prove more harmful than beneficial. That is why tantric practices are called secret Dharma, or secret way of life.

One should be aware that in tantric literature there is great praise of the monastic vows and the related ethical guidelines of the prātimokṣa.[51] For example, the *Root Tantra of Kālacakra* (*Śrīkālacakranāmatantrarāja*), the king of all tantras of Highest Yoga Tantra, mentions that among vajra masters granting tantric teachings and ceremonies, a fully ordained monk, possessing all the monastic prātimokṣa vows, is the highest vajra master; a person possessing the monastic vows of a novice monk is a vajra master of the intermediate level; and a person who does not possess any of the monastic vows is the lowest level of vajra master.[52] Thus, there are three types of vajra master. Unlike the bodhisattva vows, which can be taken by oneself in front of a representation of the Buddha, it is necessary to receive the prātimokṣa and tantric vows from a living person, from a guru. In addition, in order to progress successfully along the tantric path, the guru from whom one receives inspiration and blessings must be part of an uninterrupted lineage, traceable back to Vajradhara Buddha himself. This is necessary in order for the empowerment ceremony, as conducted by the guru, to activate the latent potentialities in our minds and enable us to actualize the resultant state of buddhahood. Thus, in tantra the guru becomes very important.

Since the guru is such an important element in the practice of tantra, the tantric writings prescribe many qualifications of the tantric master. While a tantric master who confers an empowerment ceremony should, in fact, possess the necessary qualifications, it is also important for the disciple to examine whether this person, whom one is interested in taking on as a guru, actually possesses these qualifications or not. This point has been very strongly emphasized; it is often said that you should make a thorough examination of a potential guru, even should it take twelve years.

Regarding some of the recommended qualifications for a vajra master in tantra, he or she should be a person who guards his or her three doors of body, speech, and mind from negative actions; who is "tamed" and gentle; who is well versed in the knowledge of the *Three Baskets* (*Tripiṭaka*), and well practiced in their subject matter—the three higher trainings of morality, concentration, and wisdom; and who possesses the two sets of ten principles, inner and outer.[53]

The *Gurupañcāśikā* (*Fifty Verses on the Guru*) describes a person who is not qualified to be a tantric master as someone who is lacking in compassion or is hateful; who possesses strong attachment, hatred, jealousy, and so on; who has no knowledge of the three higher trainings; and who is boastful of the little knowledge he or she possesses. Such a person should not be taken as a tantric master.[54] Just as a tantric master should possess certain qualifications, the same is true of tantric disciples. There is a current tendency among Dharma practitioners to be too eager to attend initiations given by any lama without any critical investigation. Afterwards, when things do not work out well, they easily speak badly of the lama. This, I think, is not a good habit.

On the guru's part, it is important to present the teachings in accordance with the general structure of the Buddhist path, by using the framework of the Buddhist path as a yardstick by which one determines the straightness of one's teachings. The point here is that the teacher should not be arrogant, feeling like an almighty god or creator amongst his or her close circle of disciples, thinking, "I can do anything I like!" There is a Tibetan saying: "Even if your mental level equals that of the devas, you must still behave like a human."

This, then, is a brief explanation about initiation.

17

PLEDGES AND VOWS

ONCE YOU HAVE TAKEN AN EMPOWERMENT, you have a great responsibility—a heavy burden!—to observe certain pledges and vows. In the first two classes of tantra, Action and Performance Tantra, though one must observe the bodhisattva vows, there is no need to take the tantric vows. In any tantra where there is a vajra master initiation, however, it becomes necessary to observe the tantric vows.

If one is emphasizing the practice of the three lower tantras, it is crucial to maintain a vegetarian diet. Vegetarianism is very admirable. In the case of those living in Tibet in the past, because of the climatic conditions and the scarcity of green vegetables, it is perhaps understandable that people generally adopted a non-vegetarian diet. Now, however, particularly in countries where there is an abundance of fresh vegetables and fruits, it is far better to reduce our consumption of non-vegetarian food as much as possible. Especially if you are entertaining a large gathering of people at festivals or parties, it is very good if you can arrange for vegetarian dishes to be served at such social occasions. There is a Tibetan story: Once, a nomad came to visit Lhasa, where he saw people eating a lot of vegetables. He was so surprised that when he returned home, he commented that one should never fear that the people of Lhasa would die of starvation—they eat anything that is green!

The general Buddhist stand on the question of vegetarianism, even from the perspective of the Vinaya, is that, apart from a few specific situations, there is no unequivocal prohibition against

eating meat. This is the prevailing view in such Buddhist countries as Sri Lanka, Burma, and Thailand, as reflected in the dietary
habits of the Buddhist monks from these countries. However, in
the scriptural collections of the Mahayana—the Bodhisattva
Vehicle—taking non-vegetarian food is generally proscribed. Yet,
although there is this general proscription, it is not always followed strictly. We find that in his *Madhyamaka-hṛdayakārikā*
(*Essence of the Middle Way*),[55] Bhāvaviveka raises the question of
vegetarianism and its importance for the Buddhist way of life.
He reasons that since at the time of actually taking the food the
animal has already died, the act of eating it does not constitute
any direct harm to a sentient being. What is specifically prohibited is taking any meat or non-vegetarian food that you have
ordered having the knowledge, or even the suspicion, that it has
been killed especially for you. Such meat should not be eaten.

In the three lower classes of tantra, taking non-vegetarian
food is strictly prohibited. In Highest Yoga Tantra, however,
practitioners are actually advised to rely upon the five types of
meat and the five types of nectar.[56] The perfect practitioner of
Highest Yoga Tantra is an individual of such high faculties that,
through the power of meditative concentration, he or she is able
to transform the five meats and the five nectars into purified
substances, thus rendering them usable to increase the fuel of
blissful energy within the body. In this regard, someone might
try to justify eating meat on the grounds that he or she is a practitioner of Highest Yoga Tantra. But this person must not forget
that included in the five nectars and five meats are substances
that are normally considered dirty and repulsive. A true practitioner of Highest Yoga Tantra does not discriminate by taking
the meat but not the dirty substances, but we cover our noses if
such dirty substances are anywhere near us, let alone actually
ingesting them.

At this point, I would also like to address the issue of gender
in Buddhism, especially the attitudes towards women. In Vinaya

practice—that is, the monastic way of life—male and female practitioners are granted equal opportunities for the various levels of ordination. We have male lay practitioners and female lay practitioners, novice monks and nuns, and finally, of course, fully ordained monks and nuns. Although equal opportunities are given to both male and female practitioners to take these monastic vows, we do find that fully ordained monks are regarded as superior objects of respect and veneration, compared to fully ordained nuns. From this, one might say there exists some discrimination. Also, in the writings of the Hinayana, we find passages that state that the bodhisattva on the highest level of the path, who is at the threshold of full enlightenment—that is, the bodhisattva who will definitely attain full enlightenment within his lifetime—can only be a male.[57] Similar statements can also be found in certain Mahayana sutras as well as in the literature belonging to all three lower classes of tantra. But the position of Highest Yoga Tantra is different. Here, even at the beginning, receiving an empowerment is possible only on the basis of a profound experience of sexual union. This means that both male and female deities must be present in a mandala—that is, both the dhyāni buddhas and the dhyāni consorts must exist together in the visualized mandala. Also, in the context of the pledges and commitments to be maintained following an initiation, the nature of one's relationship to women is especially emphasized in Highest Yoga Tantra. For example, despising women is an infraction of one of the root vows of tantra, but the tantras do not speak of transgressing a root vow if one despises men! Male practitioners may have difficulty understanding this obvious discrimination.

Also, in the actual meditational practice, or *sādhana,* of the mandala deities, in many of the Mother Tantras—such as the *Vajrayoginī Tantra*—the principal deity of the mandala is in female aspect.

When practitioners reach the higher levels of the tantric path, it is recommended that they seek a consort as an impetus for further progress on the path. When this union takes place, if the male practitioner is more advanced in his realization, he is able to assist his partner in bringing about the actualization of the various resultant states. This is also true if the female practitioner is more advanced: she too is able to assist her male partner in attaining the higher states. Thus, the effects are complementary, whatever the gender of the practitioner.

Hence, in Highest Yoga Tantra—for example, in the *Guhyasamāja Root Tantra*—the possibility of a female practitioner becoming fully enlightened in her lifetime in female form is stated explicitly and unambiguously. Basically, this is possible because in tantra, and specifically in Highest Yoga Tantra, the practitioner engages in a method of exploring and developing the latent potentiality within herself, especially the fundamental innate mind of clear light. From the point of view of possessing this fundamental innate mind, there is no difference between men and women. As a consequence, there is no difference between them with regard to attaining the resultant state as well. Therefore, from the ultimate viewpoint in Buddhism, that of Highest Yoga Tantra, there is no discrimination based on gender.

18

TANTRIC PRACTICE:
THE FIRST THREE CLASSES OF TANTRA

I WOULD NOW LIKE TO EXPLAIN the actual path of tantric practice. In the lower classes of tantra, two levels of path are mentioned. Technically, these are called the yoga with signs and the yoga without signs. Again, Action Tantra also presents its path from another perspective, that is, in terms of the methods of actualizing the body, speech, and mind of the resultant buddhahood: the path of actualizing the enlightened body is known as visualizing the deity; the path of actualizing enlightened speech is explained as mantra repetition—whispered mantra repetition and mental repetition; and the path of actualizing the enlightened mind is known technically as the concentration that bestows liberation at the end of sound. This type of concentration requires the prerequisite concentrations technically called the concentration abiding in fire and the concentration abiding in sound.[58]

There are differing opinions among tantric masters as to whether the practice of Action Tantra includes the practice of self-generation as the deity or not. The prevailing view is that, generally speaking, there is no necessity for trainees of Action Tantra to generate themselves as the deity, since meditation on the deity can be confined to visualizing the deity in front of the practitioner. However, the principal trainees of Action Tantra are those who can actually generate themselves as the deity and visualize the deity on that basis.

The process of visualizing the deity, as explained in Action Tantra, is done through the six-step meditation of generating the deity. These six steps, designed for the principal trainees of Action Tantra, are (1) emptiness, (2) sound, (3) letter, (4) form, (5) seal, and (6) the deity of sign, or symbol.

In this context, the deity of emptiness, or the ultimate deity, refers to contemplation of the emptiness of oneself and the deity. In meditation, one reflects on the empty nature common to both the deity and oneself. As Āryadeva explains in his *Catuḥśataka*,[59] from the standpoint of ultimate nature, there is no difference whatsoever between all the varied appearances of phenomena. They are all equal in lacking inherent existence, and therefore, they are of "one taste." This is why we can speak of the multiple and diverse as becoming of a single taste. Although all phenomena have identical empty natures, on the conventional level they manifest in many different forms and appearances. Thus, we can speak of diversity arising from unity.

The second step is the deity of sound. From within the sphere of emptiness—that uniform ultimate nature of oneself and the deity—one imagines the deity and oneself resounding the sound of mantra. This is not in the form of a letter but, instead, is mere sound. Maintaining this contemplation is the second step, the deity of sound.

In the third step, the deity of letter, the practitioner visualizes that from within that state of self-resounding mantra and at one's own place, the mantra appears in the shape of letters, standing on a white moon disc.

The fourth step is the form deity, in which the meditator actually generates the form of the deity from the letters of the mantra. This is followed by the next step, the deity of seal, or mudrā. After having generated oneself as the deity, the practitioner performs specific and appropriate mudrās, or symbolic hand gestures.[60] In the case of the lotus lineage, for example, one performs the appropriate hand gesture at the heart. This would constitute the deity of mudrā.

The last step is the deity of the symbol. This refers to the process where, having performed the symbolic hand gestures, one visualizes the three parts of the body—crown, throat, and heart—as marked by the three seed syllables, OM, ĀḤ, and HŪM. Then wisdom beings are invited to enter your body. This is the last step, the deity of the symbol.

In all Buddhist tantric practices, before generating oneself into the deity, the practitioner must meditate on emptiness. On every occasion, before generating oneself into a deity, whether or not the *sādhana*[61] begins with the Sanskrit expressions, OM SVABHĀVAŚUDDHĀ SARVADHARMĀ SVABHĀVAŚUDDHO 'HAM or OM ŚŪNYATĀ JÑĀNA VAJRA SVABHĀVĀTMAKO 'HAM and so forth, you should always meditate on emptiness. This signifies that you are generating your own wisdom, your consciousness realizing emptiness, into the appearance of the deity. In the beginning, this takes place only at the level of your imagination. Still, this serves as a form of rehearsal that prepares you for the eventual experience when your own wisdom realizing emptiness actually arises in the form of a deity. Therefore, if you lack an understanding of emptiness as expounded either by the Yogācāra or the Madhyamaka school, then a successful practice of tantric yoga becomes extremely difficult. The appearance of the deity generated from your own wisdom realizing emptiness constitutes the *vast wheel of the deity* or the *method factor of the path*. Not only that, but the practitioner must also periodically reaffirm his or her awareness and mindfulness of the empty nature of the generated deity. This, in brief, is the meditation on *Mahāmudrā*, or the Great Seal, which, according to Action Tantra, ripens the practitioner's faculties to actualize the Form Body of an enlightened being.

If the meditator has not attained single-pointed calm abiding, but is cultivating *śamatha* in conjunction with tantric practice, then he or she should focus on developing single-pointedness after generating the deity and before the mantra repetition. Thus, at this point in the sādhana, one undertakes meditation. Many tantric manuals and ritual texts recommend that when you feel tired of such meditation, or if you begin to doze off, you should change from meditation to mantra repetition. For those who perform intensive mantra repetition but no meditation at all, when you feel tired, then there is nothing to do but end the session! In the texts and meditation manuals, the primary emphasis is on meditation while mantra repetition remains secondary.

Action Tantra speaks of two types of mantra repetition. The first is whispered mantra repetition, in which you recite the mantra in a quiet manner, so that you can just barely hear it yourself. The second is mental repetition, in which you do not pronounce the mantra at all but only mentally imagine the mantra sound.

In the context of one's meditation on the sādhana, Action Tantra mentions two paths of training, the profound and the vast. Training in the profound path refers to a special, unique meditation on emptiness, that is, the meditation on the empty nature of the visualized deity. Focusing thus on the empty nature of the deity constitutes the profound practice. Training in the vast path consists of two aspects. First, you seek to develop the clear appearance of the deity. Then, on the basis of a firm and clear appearance of yourself as the deity, you endeavor to develop divine pride, or [self-]identity. In other words, having first generated the clear visualization of yourself as the deity, you then develop a strong sense of divine pride of yourself as the deity.

The Indian master Buddhaśrījñāna, in one of his meditation manuals,[62] raises the question: Since ignorance is the root cause of our life in this vicious cycle of existence, and since we do not find, in Generation Stage deity yoga, any explicit meditation on emptiness, how can we maintain that deity yoga serves as an opponent force eliminating the root cause, ignorance? Buddhaśrījñāna responds by stating that in the Generation Stage of tantra, deity yoga is the practice wherein one meditates on the empty nature of the form of the deity. Thus, one does not merely visualize the deity, but instead one meditates upon the emptiness of the deity while maintaining that divine appearance and visualization. Hence, in the practice of deity yoga, we find that there are two aspects: deity yoga focusing on the conventional nature, or the appearance of the deity, and deity yoga focusing on the ultimate nature, or the emptiness of the deity.

Tantra also speaks of three types of behavioral attitudes: (1) all appearances as divine mandala deities and supporting environment; (2) all sounds as mantras; and (3) all conscious experiences and awareness as various aspects of the non-dual wisdom of the deity. The first type of attitude—imagining everything that appears as the divine body and supporting mandala of the deity—should be understood as a perception to be developed for a very specific purpose, rather than out of belief in its correspondence to reality, this purpose being to overcome our sense of ordinariness. On the level of our imagination, we try to develop the ability to perceive all appearances as divine forms of the deity; by doing so, our apprehension of any thought remains always within the context of emptiness.

However, there is a divergent opinion that maintains that such attitudes are not mere imaginative states but true understandings that accord with the actual state of affairs. According to the *Lam-dre* practice in the Sakya tradition, the meaning of tantra, or "continuum," is explained in terms of the *three tantras*.[63] The first, causal tantra, refers to the fundamental basis, which is the source of both samsara and nirvana and at which level they are also equal. In order to obtain a perception of everything as being pure and divine, the practitioner is introduced to the view of the indivisibility of samsara and nirvana, and thereby, to the nature of the fundamental basis.

Similarly, the great Dzog-chen master Dodrup Jigme Tenpai Nyima in his *General Exposition of Guhyagarbha* (*gSang snying spyi don*), states that the cultivation of this pure perception—

that is, the view that all things and events that appear and occur in samsara and nirvana, are, in fact, manifestations, "sport" or "play," of the fundamental basis—is, according to specific Nyingma terminology, called *rig-pa,* or pristine awareness. This pristine awareness is the basis, the source; everything that occurs and appears in the expanse of reality—samsara and nirvana—is a manifestation, or "sport," of awareness. Pristine awareness, then, is identified with the subtlest level of clear light.

Madhyamaka philosophy also speaks of emptiness as the origin of all conventional phenomena. Emptiness is, in some sense, like a creator since all phenomena can be seen as different manifestations of this underlying ultimate nature. In the same way, according to the explanations of the Sakya tradition and that of the Nyingma master Dodrup Jigme Tenpai Nyima, all phenomena occurring and appearing in the cycle of existence and in nirvana are manifestations, or "sport," of the pristine awareness, or fundamental basis. This awareness—in other words, the subtle mind of clear light—is eternal in terms of its continuity, and its essential nature is unpolluted by the delusions. Therefore, it is essentially pure and clear. From that point of view, there is the possibility of extending our view of purity to include all phenomena, which are actually manifestations, or "play," of the fundamental basis. We must remember, however, that these two profound explanations are given from the viewpoint of Highest Yoga Tantra.

At this point in the sādhana practice, you should engage in profound meditation along the lines just described. When you begin to feel exhausted, or if your meditation starts to become mixed with sleep, you should then move on to the next stage, the mantra repetition.

We have discussed different types of mantra repetition, such as whispered mantra repetition and mental mantra repetition, as methods for actualizing enlightened speech. There are also methods for actualizing enlightened mind: for example, the concentrations called abiding in fire, abiding in sound, and bestowing liberation at the end of sound.

The *concentration of abiding in fire* is a meditation in which the practitioner visualizes different mantras and seed syllables at the heart of the meditational deity and imagines flames emerging from these mantra syllables. The *concentration of abiding in sound* is a meditation in which the emphasis is placed primarily on the tone of the mantra recitation. The practitioner imagines and concentrates on the tone of the mantra as if listening to the mantra being recited by another, rather than by oneself. In this way, the practitioner cultivates single-pointedness, or tranquil abiding, by focusing on the tone. In Action Tantra, we find passages that tell us that through the practice of the concentration of abiding in fire, the practitioner will develop physical and mental suppleness. Then, through meditation on the concentration of abiding in sound, the practitioner attains tranquil abiding, or single-pointedness of the mind. The third type of yoga is technically called *bestowing liberation at the end of sound*. It is through the practice of this last meditative technique that the tantric practitioner will eventually attain liberation according to the tantras of the Action and Performance classes.

If we were to place the tantric teachings into one of the three scriptural collections—discipline, sets of discourses, and metaphysical knowledge—they would be included in the sets of discourses. In tantra, the Buddha himself said that he would teach tantra following the style of the sutra teachings. This indicates that the unique feature common to all four classes of tantra that distinguishes tantric practice from its sutra counterparts emerges in the special techniques for cultivating meditative stabilization since this is the main subject of the sets of discourses.

Generally speaking, tranquil abiding is an absorptive meditative state of mind in which the practitioner is able to maintain his or her focus of attention on a chosen object single-pointedly. The techniques, therefore, for cultivating such a state must correspondingly be absorptive rather than analytic. Special insight, on the other hand, is an analytic type of meditation, and therefore the methods for cultivating special insight must correspondingly be analytic in nature.

Tranquil, or calm, abiding is a heightened state of awareness possessing a very single-pointed nature, accompanied by faculties of mental and physical suppleness. Your body and mind become especially flexible, receptive, and serviceable. Special insight is a heightened state of awareness, also accompanied by mental and physical suppleness, in which your faculty of analysis is immensely advanced. Thus, calm abiding is absorptive in nature, whereas special insight is analytic in nature.

We must, when speaking about meditation, be aware that there are many different types of meditation. Certain types of meditation take something as their object—for example, the meditation on emptiness in which emptiness is taken as the object of the meditative mind. In other types, the practitioner generates the mind into a certain state, such as meditation on love, in which the practitioner generates love within the mind. The term meditation has different connotations. In other instances, the practitioner visualizes something on an imaginary level and meditates on that. These are a few of the different types of meditation.

According to the explanations in the sutras and the three lower tantras, the attainment of calm abiding and special insight is always sequential. First, you must attain calm abiding, and then it will lead to special insight. Also, when you cultivate calm abiding during a meditation session, you do so solely in an absorptive manner—that is, you maintain single-pointedness without applying analysis—and when you cultivate special insight, you do so predominantly through an analytic process. Thus, they are regarded as two distinct and independent processes.

However, Highest Yoga Tantra has a unique method of pinpointing and penetrating certain vital points of the subtle physical body in meditation, thereby giving rise to the attainment of special insight through a predominantly absorptive meditation. Thus, some practitioners with high mental faculties are able to attain the two realizations, tranquil abiding and special insight, simultaneously rather than sequentially.

The third type of yoga referred to above, the concentration of bestowing liberation at the end of sound, is the technical term given to the meditation on emptiness according to the lower tantric systems. This meditation is also known as the yoga without signs, whereas the first two concentrations and their preceding meditations are called the yoga with signs. In Action Tantra, the yoga without signs refers to the meditation on and realization of emptiness.

I also want to speak a little about Performance Tantra. The mandalas belonging to this class of tantra are quite rare in the Tibetan tradition. The most popular deity belonging to this class of tantra in the Tibetan tradition is Vairocanābhisaṃbodhi.

Performance Tantra also speaks of the path to buddhahood in terms of the yoga with signs and the yoga without signs. In this context, the meditation, or yoga, where the emphasis is on the practice of emptiness is the yoga without signs, whereas, in the yoga with signs, the emphasis is *not* on the practice of emptiness.

In both Action and Performance Tantras, the required practices are deity yoga and undertaking the "approximation," or meditation in a retreat situation, followed by engaging in the various designated activities associated with that deity's practice. These activities, which are mentioned in the Action and Performance Tantras and are engaged in by practitioners after having done the approximation in retreat, consist of certain actions, such as cultivating immortality and longevity on the basis of the long life deities, and so forth. However, in the literature of this class of tantra, other activities, such as reaching the highest form of liberation and so on, are not discussed in detail.

The chief deity in Yoga Tantra—that is, the third class in the fourfold division—whose tantra is translated into the Tibetan language, is Vajradhātu; also included is the tantra of Vairocana. With regard to Yoga Tantra, the general mode of procedure is explained in terms of three aspects: the basis of purification, the purifying path, and the purified results. The basis of purification here refers to the body, speech, mind, and conduct of the practitioner. The purifying path refers to the practice of the four seals: the great seal, the seal of phenomena, the wisdom seal, and the action seal. Hence, just as there are four bases of purification, there are four corresponding purifying paths. The purified results are the body, speech, mind, and activities of buddhahood.

Accordingly, we find that Yoga Tantra has a root tantra composed of four sections called *Compendium of Principles* (*Sarvatathāgatatattvasaṃgraha*). In this category of tantra, the style of presentation is mostly on the basis of this fourfold approach. Although I have received initiations belonging to this class of tantra, I do not have much realization myself of this particular class as I have not done sufficient meditative practice associated with these tantras. So perhaps it is better if I leave the discussion at this point!

19

ADVANCED TANTRIC PRACTICE:
HIGHEST YOGA TANTRA

GENERAL INTRODUCTION

FOR US TIBETANS, HIGHEST YOGA TANTRA is like our daily diet, and thus we are more familiar with this class of tantra. The practices of Vajradhātu and Vairocanābhisaṃbodhi are flourishing in Japan, so it would seem that there are many practitioners of the lower classes of tantra there. But it seems that only in the Tibetan tradition do we find the practice of Highest Yoga Tantra. However, I cannot be completely sure of this. The principal trainees for whom Highest Yoga Tantra was primarily intended are the human beings of this planet, belonging to the desire realm, whose physical bodies are composed of six vital constituents. These six constituents are the three—bone, marrow, and regenerative fluid—obtained from the father and the three—flesh, skin, and blood—obtained from the mother.[64]

A unique characteristic of the paths of Highest Yoga Tantra is that it employs in its profound path various meditative techniques that have corresponding similitudes not only to the resultant state of buddhahood, that is, to the three kāyas,[65] but especially to the bases of purification on the ordinary level of human existence—for example, death, intermediate state, and rebirth.

Moreover, as alluded to earlier, the meaning of tantra acquires a greater profundity in Highest Yoga Tantra in that it is understood from the perspective of three scopes known as the three tantras. These are: (1) causal tantra—the basis; (2) method tantra—the path; and (3) resultant tantra—the fruit. All three levels of tantra ultimately arise from the fundamental innate mind of clear light.

The significance of this, when understood correctly, is that one appreciates the unique presentation of the Sakya tradition when it speaks of causal tantra—called the basis of all, or fundamental basis—by which it refers to the residential mandala and the resident deities. All of them actually arise from this fundamental basis. According to this presentation, within this fundamental basis—that is, within this basic faculty that we all possess—all phenomena of the base, the ordinary level, are present in the form of their characteristics; all phenomena on the path are present in the form of enlightened qualities; and all phenomena of the resultant state of buddhahood are present in the form of potential.

Similarly, because of the above, we find in the writings of the Nyingma, or Old Translation, schools such expressions as "equanimity of the base and the result." Since all phenomena belonging to the resultant state are present and complete within the fundamental basis in the form of potential, we can comprehend such statements as "the exalted body and the exalted wisdom can neither be conjoined nor individuated." By the body and wisdom of an enlightened being are meant the two kāyas—rūpakāya, or Form Body, and dharmakāya, or Truth Body.

We should keep such meanings and points in mind as the ultimate intent when we read in Maitreya's *Uttaratantra* that the defilements of the mind are circumstantial and adventitious, whereas the positive qualities of the mind are naturally present within it.[66] This does not mean that all the positive qualities and realizations of the mind are already present within the mind. Rather, they are there in the form of potential within the fundamental innate mind of clear light. It is, therefore, important to understand these expressions and their related concepts carefully and correctly, otherwise there is the danger of holding a misconception similar to that of the non-Buddhist Sāṃkhya school, which maintains that a sprout is present at the time of its seed (but that it is invisible).

It is also from such points of view that we can understand statements asserting that if you recognize yourself properly, you are fully enlightened. We also find other similar passages in tantra. In the *Hevajra Tantra* we find, "...although sentient beings are fully enlightened, still, they are obscured by adventitious defilements...." The *Kālacakra Tantra* also speaks emphatically about the fundamental innate mind of clear light, but it does so using different terminology, calling it instead the *all-pervading vajra space.*

It is for such reasons that in his *Pañcakrama* (*Five Stages*), a commentary on the five Completion Stages of the *Guhyasamāja Tantra*, Nāgārjuna mentions that the practitioner, while abiding in the illusory meditation, perceives all phenomena in the same aspect.[67] The implication here is that a practitioner on the Completion Stage, when able to arise in the very subtle body—technically called the *illusory body*, which is in the nature of the subtlest energy and mind—extends his perception to encompass all phenomena, he perceives them as manifestations, that is, the sport or play, of the fundamental innate mind of clear light.

It may be reasonable to perceive all living beings as manifestations or sport of the fundamental innate mind of clear light, since eventually it is from this fundamental source that all living beings have arisen; therefore, it is the origin. We may ask, however, how we are supposed to understand the entire universe, including the natural environment, as being a manifestation or play of this fundamental innate mind of clear light. We certainly need not perceive this in the same manner as the Cittamātra, or Mind Only school, maintaining that the environment and external phenomena have no reality other than as mere projections of the mind. This Buddhist school of thought views all external phenomena as nothing more than reflections of our own mind, and denies any atomically structured external reality.

Here, in Nāgārjuna's *Pañcakrama,* the meaning is slightly different. The environment and external phenomena should be understood as manifestations, or appearances, of this fundamental mind, rather than being in the nature of that mind. When a person manifestly experiences this fundamental innate mind of clear light, the most subtle level of mind, all the gross mental processes and the corresponding energies have dissolved, or withdrawn, and so are no longer functioning. That which appears to this subtle mind is referred to as *pure emptiness* because it resembles the experience, or state, of meditative equipoise directly realizing emptiness.

Highest Yoga Tantra explains different techniques for utilizing the fundamental innate mind of clear light, which manifests naturally at the time of death. One can use this mind for positive purposes by generating it into a virtuous thought or into an aspect of the path. In the sutra system, this last subtle moment of consciousness, the consciousness at the time of death, is generally said to be invariably neutral, neither virtuous nor non-virtuous. But in tantra, there are methods of utilizing that last moment of consciousness so that it does not remain neutral but is instead generated into a virtuous state.

It is said that in comparison to negative states of mind, virtuous states are far more powerful since they have valid bases of support, and are reasoned and unmistaken. Moreover, virtuous states of mind can be generated and prolonged at the time of death or during other occasions when the clear light experience naturally occurs; on the other hand, negative states of mind cannot become manifest or remain present at the time of death or at any other time when the clear light state is manifested.

Both the view of Mahāmudrā, or Great Seal, in the Kagyu tradition and the view of breakthrough practice in the Great Perfection school[68] come down to the same point: the experience of the fundamental innate mind of clear light. In the Nyingma presentation of the nine vehicles, the Great Perfection, or Dzog-chen, is presented as the peak of all vehicles. It is considered to be the highest because in the practice of Great Perfection we utilize our pristine awareness rather than utilizing our ordinary mind as in the preceding eight vehicles. Yet, if this is the case, how can we explain that these various views—whether of Mahāmudrā, Dzog-chen breakthrough practice, or Highest Yoga Tantra—come to the same point: the fundamental innate mind of clear light?

An answer to this question has been given by Dodrup Jigme Tenpai Nyima, who states that it is indeed true that Highest Yoga Tantra strongly emphasizes exploring and developing the fundamental innate mind of clear light, as do the Great Perfection teachings. However, the difference lies in methodology. In Highest Yoga Tantra practice, techniques of exploring and developing this fundamental mind are explained in a gradual process beginning with the Generation Stage and eventually leading to the subsequent Completion Stages of meditation and the actualization of the clear light. In contrast, the development and enhancement of this fundamental mind of clear light is not approached in a gradual process in the practice of Great Perfection but, instead, is approached immediately, as if one is directly apprehending the clear light mind itself, right from the beginning, through utilizing one's pristine awareness.

DECIPHERING THE TANTRAS: THE INTERPRETIVE KEYS

We should always remember when studying Highest Yoga Tantra that even a single word has many different levels of interpretation, similar to the way in which the wisdom sutras have two levels of interpretation—the explicit meaning and the hidden meaning. In fact, in the case of the tantras, the interpretive process must go much deeper, encompassing many different levels with an even greater degree of complexity.

A single word or expression in tantra can have four different meanings, corresponding to the four levels of interpretation known as the *four modes of understanding*, which are (1) the literal meaning, (2) the general meaning, (3) the hidden meaning, and (4) the ultimate meaning.[69]

The first, the literal meaning, refers to the explicit meaning of statements, which can be understood on the basis of literary conventions and the grammatical structure of the sentence. On the other hand, the second, the general meaning refers to the level of meaning related to the meditative practices and the mode of procedure common to the lower tantras. Thus, in this context, *general* has a connotation of commonality. With regard to the third, there are three types of hidden meaning: (1) the concealed method of taking desire into the path; (2) the concealed appearances, for example, the white appearance, red increase, and black near-attainment;[70] and (3) the concealed conventional truth, the illusory body. Although these are important subjects of the scriptures of the Highest Yoga Tantra, they are nevertheless not explicit in the lower tantras but hinted at in a concealed manner. The fourth mode is the ultimate meaning. *Ultimate* here refers to the clear light and the profound union that are the ultimate objects of all the scriptures and practices of Highest Yoga Tantra.

The tantras also mention another hermeneutical device that can help us in approaching a text of Highest Yoga Tantra. This is the recognition of the *six parameters*. They refer to three pairs of antitheses that naturally circumscribe the meaningfulness of a text: (1) the parameters of the interpretable and the definitive; (2) the parameters of the intended and the unintended; and (3) the parameters of the literal and the non-literal.

As a consequence of this multi-layered approach to understanding tantric texts and instructions, when tantra is actually taught to disciples, there are two styles of explanation: the kind of explanation given in a teaching to a gathering of disciples and the kind given in the context of a teacher-pupil relationship.

As a way of authenticating the practice of tantra as a genuine Buddhist practice leading to the eventual attainment of buddhahood, tantric treatises always present their subject matter in accord with and based on the mode of procedure of the sutra path. All the subtle complexities and differences in the various tantras arise in response to differences in mental disposition, natural inclinations, and physical characteristics of practitioners. This is why most tantras are prefaced with a preliminary section dealing primarily with the appropriate qualifications and credentials necessary for a practitioner. Different types of practitioners are mentioned, the best type being the "jewel-like" practitioner. The purpose of explaining tantra to the appropriate trainees in such a complex manner is to enable each trainee to realize the two truths. The two truths referred to here are not the two truths explained in the sutra system but the ultimate and conventional truths according to Highest Yoga Tantra. This mode of approaching and interpreting a tantric text or treatise is discussed in extensive detail in the explanatory tantra called the *Wisdom Vajra Compendium* (*Jñānavajrasamuccayanāmatantra*).

Another distinctive feature of the tantras is that nearly all begin with the two syllables: E and VAM. These two syllables encompass the entire essence and meaning of all the tantras, not just their literal meaning but also their definitive meaning. Every tantra, as a treatise, is composed of many different syllables, all of which can ultimately be reduced to vowels and consonants. Therefore, all syllables are contained in the two syllables of E-VAM. Since the entire meaning of tantra can be condensed into the three factors of base, path, and result, all aspects of base, path, and result are contained in the meaning of E-VAM as well. Thus, E-VAM actually comprises the entire subject matter of tantra.

In like fashion, Candrakīrti succinctly summarizes the entire meaning of tantra in the opening verses of his well-known commentary on the *Guhyasamāja Tantra* entitled *Pradīpoddyotananāmaṭīkā* (*Clear Lamp*).[71] In these verses, Candrakīrti writes that in order to actualize the deity body, the first stage in tantric practice is the Generation Stage; meditation on the nature of mind is the second stage; attaining a stable conventional truth is the third stage; and purification of the conventional truth is the fourth stage. The fifth stage is conjoining the two truths: this is called union. These are the branches of tantra. In essence, they encompass the entire subject matter of Highest Yoga Tantra.[72]

Candrakīrti's treatise explains the entire tantric path in terms of five stages: first, the Generation Stage, and then, the four stages of completion, as mentioned above. Just as there are different stages on the path, there are also different initiations, which are the corresponding ripening factors for these paths. The initiation that empowers the practitioner to undertake the practice of the Generation Stage is the vase initiation. The second initiation, the secret initiation, is that which empowers the practitioner to engage in the practice of the illusory body. The path of the illusory body also includes the three isolations: the meditative stabilizations of the isolated body, isolated speech, and isolated mind. These are preliminaries to the practice of the illusory body. With the third initiation, the wisdom-knowledge initiation, the practitioner is empowered to undertake the meditation on clear light, which purifies the illusory body into clear light. And with the fourth initiation, the word initiation, the practitioner is empowered to undertake the meditative practices of union.

BLISS AND EMPTINESS

Generally speaking, there are two principal ways in which the term *union* is used in Highest Yoga Tantra: the union of the two truths, and the union of bliss and emptiness. In the context of the union of the two truths, the indivisible union of bliss and emptiness, described below, is itself a single entity—ultimate truth, which is unified with the illusory body— conventional truth. When these two are inseparably conjoined, one has achieved the perfect union of the two truths.

The union of bliss and emptiness refers to an indivisible union between the wisdom realizing emptiness and a profound experience of bliss. In such a union, the previously gained wisdom that realizes emptiness is generated within a blissful state of mind; thus, these two—wisdom and bliss—are experienced within a single entity of consciousness. This union could also result from utilizing a profound experience of bliss to newly realize emptiness. In other words, there are two possible sequences for attaining a union of bliss and emptiness. Some practitioners might experience a blissful state of mind as a result of melting the vital drops within the energy channels, with this blissful experience eventually leading to the realization of emptiness. For the main practitioners of Highest Yoga Tantra, however, the realization of emptiness precedes the actual experience of great bliss.

Some practitioners may have a view of emptiness which is not as complete as that of the Madhyamaka-Prāsaṅgika school, but is closer to the views propounded by the Yogācāra or Madhyamaka-Svātantrika schools. By applying certain meditative techniques of tantra, such as igniting the inner heat or penetrating the vital points of the body through wind yoga, the practitioner can experience a melting of the elements within the body that induces an experience of bliss—eventually reaching a state where one is able to dissolve the gross levels of mind and the corresponding energies. With this deep level of meditative experience conjoined with even an incomplete understanding of emptiness, the practitioner may be able to progress to a more subtle understanding of emptiness, eventually perceiving that every phenomenon is a mere mental imputation, a mere designation imputed on a base. The experience of great bliss may help the practitioner to perceive all things and events as mere manifestations of bliss, or the "play" of the subtle wind. In this way, the meditator can realize the most subtle experience of emptiness. For that type of person, the experience of bliss is attained first, and the realization of emptiness comes later.

Generally, a practitioner should have achieved a realization of emptiness before being initiated into Highest Yoga Tantra. In this case, the wisdom realizing emptiness is attained before the experience of bliss. Such a practitioner of superior faculties, during the actual meditative session on the "self" or "I," utilizes the methods of igniting the inner heat, practicing deity yoga, or penetrating the vital points of the body through manipulating the subtle energies and so on. The meditator melts the drops, the essential elements within the body, and through the force of the desire originally generated, experiences a great state of bliss. At this point, the meditator re-cognizes the earlier experience of emptiness and conjoins this realization with the experience of great bliss.

How do you generate such an experience of great bliss? When the drops melt within your body, you experience a unique sensation originating within the central channel. This gives rise to a powerful experience of physical bliss which, in turn, brings your mind to a very subtle level of experience which is permeated by mental bliss. When you then reflect on your understanding of emptiness, this mental bliss is automatically conjoined with emptiness. This is the method of conjoining bliss and emptiness.

It is important to understand the exact meaning of each term or expression in tantra, especially given the multiplicity of meanings that vary according to different contexts. Generally, there are three distinct types of bliss: (1) the bliss caused by the emission of regenerative fluids; (2) the bliss derived from the flow of the vital elements within the energy channels; and finally, (3) the bliss known in tantra as *immutable bliss*. In tantric practice, the latter two types of bliss are those utilized for realizing emptiness: the bliss derived from the movement of the elements in the channels and immutable bliss. Because of the significance of utilizing bliss in realizing emptiness, many meditational deities in Highest Yoga Tantra are depicted in sexual embrace. As we discussed before, this bliss is very different from that experienced during ordinary sexual intercourse.

134

DEATH, INTERMEDIATE STATE, AND REBIRTH

As the practice of Highest Yoga Tantra is primarily intended for trainees who have physical bodies composed of six vital constituents, even the procedure along the path is modeled on the basis of and has features similar to the ordinary processes of death, intermediate state, and rebirth. Because of the unique physical structure of the human body, human beings on this planet naturally experience the stages of death, intermediate state, and rebirth. Death is the state in which all the gross levels of mind and energy eventually dissolve into their subtlest levels. At this point, the person experiences the clear light of death. From that state of clear light, one then assumes a subtle body known as the intermediate state, and when that intermediate state being assumes a body of a grosser level and becomes visible to others, that transition marks rebirth into a new life.

Since we naturally traverse these different states in our ordinary experience, Nāgārjuna and Āryadeva, in their commentaries on tantra and in their quintessential instructions, elucidate the techniques by which the practitioner can utilize these natural stages of death, intermediate state, and rebirth for higher purposes. Rather than experiencing these states with no control, one can control and utilize them to achieve the three resultant bodies of buddhahood—the Truth Body, the Complete Enjoyment Body, and the Emanation Body—which, respectively, have features similar to death, intermediate state, and rebirth. Therefore, in Highest Yoga Tantra, death, intermediate state, and rebirth are called the *three kāyas of the base.*

As explained in the path of Highest Yoga Tantra, any Generation Stage practice should include meditation on the three embodiments of the enlightened resultant state: buddhahood. However, in the texts of the Nyingma, or Old Translation, school, different terminology is used: the meditation on the three kāyas is called the *three meditative stabilizations*. These are: the meditative stabilization of suchness, the meditative stabilization of the appearance of all, and the causal meditative stabilization.

The Generation Stage practices common to both Yoga Tantra and Highest Yoga Tantra are often explained in terms of three meditative stabilizations: the initial stage, the supreme king of the mandala, and the supreme king of actions. These, however, are different from the three meditative stabilizations described by the Old Translation school.

In brief, meditation on the three kāyas refers to meditation in which you take the three processes of death, intermediate state, and rebirth into the path. For instance, you take death into the path as the dharmakāya, or Truth Body, by imagining the actual dying process within a meditative state. In your imagination, you dissolve and withdraw all of the processes of the mind and the corresponding wind-energies. The dying process begins with the dissolution of the elements within the body. It has eight stages, beginning with the dissolution of the earth element, then the water element, the fire element, and the wind element. These four dissolutions of the elements are followed by the experience of the next four stages: white appearance, red increase, black near-attainment, and the clear light of death. During the Generation Stage, the experiences of these dissolution processes occur only within one's imagination. However, during the Completion Stage, as the practitioner advances in realizations, he or she progressively gains deeper and more realistic experiences of these processes. The practitioner is eventually able to experience, in meditation, the actual dissolution processes—and especially the experience of the subtlest clear light—just as they will occur at the actual time of death.

Some modern scientists have been conducting research on the experiences and events that occur during the process of dying. Certain results can be obtained if one focuses such research on persons who are experiencing the death process slowly and gradually, because the signs of dissolution and so on are much more apparent and clear in these individuals. This slow and gradual process takes place naturally in, for example, a person who has been sick for a long time.

A tantric practitioner who has attained advanced realizations is able to recognize these stages in the dying process as they occur and use them for positive purposes, while at the same time maintaining awareness of and not being overwhelmed by them. This ability is the result of having undertaken meditation practice during one's lifetime. Ordinary people generally remain in the clear light of death for a maximum of about three days, but some meditators are able to remain in that state for a week or, in exceptional cases, several weeks. The external sign of remaining in the clear light state is that the person may be pronounced clinically dead, but the body does not decompose.

I have a physician friend who wanted to experiment on such meditators as they pass through the experiences of death. He left a special instrument with me for this purpose, but I find it quite ironic—in order to carry out the experiment, I have to wait for a meditator to die!

In Generation Stage practice, at the point when one is experiencing the clear light on an imaginary level, one should engage in meditative equipoise on emptiness. This is the meditation on the Truth Body—the factor that purifies ordinary death.

Just as an ordinary person, after experiencing the clear light of death, enters into the intermediate state and assumes a subtle body, the Generation Stage practitioner, after arising from meditative equipoise on emptiness, assumes a subtle body on an imaginary level. This is the meditation on the Enjoyment Body—the factor that purifies the ordinary intermediate state.

Then, just as the ordinary being leaves the intermediate state and assumes a gross physical body, thus taking rebirth in a new life, in the same manner, the Generation Stage practitioner arises from the Enjoyment Body and assumes the Emanation Body.

This meditation on the Emanation Body is the factor that purifies ordinary rebirth.

There are many different manuals explaining self-generation into a deity at the Generation Stage. In some practices there will first be the arising of the causal vajra holder who then transforms into the resultant vajra holder.[73] In other cases, the self-generation takes place through the process known as the five clarifications, or *abhisaṃbodhis*.[74] Thus, there are different methods of self-generation as the deity. In the various Generation Stage sādhanas and practices, there are many different visualizations of the deity and so on. These are all important, but the most important is the meditation on the *vast* and the *profound*, in which you cultivate the clarity of visualization conjoined with divine pride. The practitioner should, as we have already discussed, cultivate the clear appearance of the deity, and then, on that basis, cultivate divine pride, or self-identity as the deity.

The serious practitioner should always relate back to his or her own mental states and level of realization when undertaking these meditations. You should watch carefully and keep your meditation free of the influences of mental sinking and mental excitement; your meditation should be performed in a sustained and concerted manner. The greatest obstacles for attaining and maintaining single-pointedness of mind are the distractions of extraneous thoughts. These include many different mental states, such as mental scattering and various forms of excitement. Among them, the greatest obstacle of all is mental excitement. This comes about when the mind is drawn to a desirable object, or when there is too much intensity in the meditation. In order to counteract and overcome the influence of excitement, it is recommended that the meditator use techniques that relax the mind, for example, withdrawing attention from external objects in order to lower the level of intensity of the mind. One helpful technique in this regard is to reflect on the fundamentally unsatisfactory nature of samsaric existence, which helps reduce the level of excitement.

In order to develop firm and stable single-pointedness of the mind, you must also have clarity of the object. Without clarity, though you may be able to withdraw your mind from external objects, you will still not be able to achieve single-pointedness. Clarity is of two types: the clarity of the perceived object and the clarity of the perceiving awareness, that is, the subjective experience itself. The factor that interrupts our clarity of mind is mental sinking. When you notice mental sinking you need to apply techniques that raise the state of your awareness. Thus, when engaging in meditation on single-pointedness, you should monitor the state of your own mind, your mood, your temperament, and so on, judging whether there is too much intensity or alertness, or too much relaxation or laxity. You can then judge for yourself to what extent you must engage the various techniques that serve to cultivate a stable single-pointedness.

In the practice of Highest Yoga Tantra, because of the uniqueness of the object of your meditation—that is, yourself in the form of the deity—and because of the unique placement of the focus of your single-pointed attention—at various locations within your body—you are able to bring about a movement of the vital elements within the body. I personally know some meditators who have had mystical experiences and have told me about them. I teach them how to meditate, and I get the opportunity to listen to the accounts of their experiences. It is a rather good bargain, isn't it!

When you are able to maintain a clear image of the deity in your mind for a long period of time in a single-pointed manner, it prevents your ordinary view and ordinary concepts from arising and leads to a feeling of divine pride. Through all of these stages of meditation, it is important to maintain continual awareness of emptiness by reaffirming your original cognition of it. As a result of engaging in meditative practice in such a precise manner, you will progress to the point where you will be able to have a clear and vivid visualization of the entire mandala and the deities within it, just as if you were seeing them directly with your eyes. This marks the attainment of the first level of the Generation Stage.[75]

When, as a result of further meditation, you reach the stage where you have within a single moment of consciousness a clear visualization of even the subtle deities that have been generated from parts of your body, you have achieved the second level of the Generation Stage. Then, once you have attained a firm meditative stabilization of single-pointedness, there are different practices you can do to gain further mastery over this ability—for example, emanating deities from your heart and dissolving them back again, and so forth. Such meditations include visualizing subtle symbols, or mudrās, at the upper opening of the central channel, and subtle drops and seed syllables at the lower end of the central channel. When you reach the point of feeling exhausted from these meditations, the next step in the sādhana is mantra repetition. There are many varieties of mantra repetition in Highest Yoga Tantra: the mantra repetition of commitment, the heap of light mantra repetition, the palanquin-like mantra repetition, the wrathful mantra repetition, and so forth.

After the mantra recitation come the practices of the post-meditation period. Since a tantric practitioner should never be separated from the practice of conjoining method and wisdom in daily life, even the post-meditation period is important. Tantra speaks of different post-meditation yogas, such as the yoga of sleeping, maintaining an appropriate diet, washing, and so on. For a serious tantric meditator, there are certain practices that can be used even when urinating, defecating, and so on. The great masters say that the progress made during the meditative session should be complemented and reinforced by the practices of the post-meditation period, and vice-versa.

During the post-meditation period, you can definitely judge whether your practice during the meditative session has been successful. If you find that your way of thinking, way of life, habitual activities, and behavior during the post-meditation session do not change but remain the same in spite of years of intensive meditational practice, this is obviously not a good sign. When we take medicine, it is not the taste, color, or quantity of the medicine that matters; the important thing is the beneficial effect on our body. If in spite of having taken a certain medicine for a long time we see no effect, there is no point in continuing to take it. Regardless of whether your practice is elaborate or short, above all, it should be effective in bringing about some kind of transformation, a change for the better, within you.

THE COMPLETION STAGE

On the basis of the practice of Generation Stage deity yoga, one can engage in various activities that serve as precursors to the Completion Stages. By pursuing these advanced Generation Stage practices, the meditator begins to feel certain beneficial physical effects within his or her body. When you begin to experience these physical effects, such as the experience of great bliss induced by the melting of the vital elements and so on, this marks the attainment of the first level of the Completion Stage.

There are many different practices associated with the Completion Stage, such as the yoga of inner fire, the yoga of wind, the yoga of four joys, and so forth. The yoga of wind includes such techniques as holding the vase breath and a technique known as vajra repetition. Having progressed from the Generation Stage to the initial levels of the Completion Stage, a lay practitioner seeks further impetus on the path by engaging in sexual union with a consort. However, for the ordained practitioner with monastic vows—monks and nuns—this is not yet the time for engaging in such union.

In order to engage in the profound practices of the Completion Stage, the practitioner must first become fully acquainted with the subtle nature of the body. He or she must develop a knowledge of the stationery channels, the winds, or *prāṇas*, that flow within the channels, and the subtle drops that reside at specific locations within the body. Regarding the channels, the tantras generally refer to three main channels—the central channel, and the right and left channels—as well as the five channel centers, or *cakras*.[76] The three main channels then branch and re-branch throughout the body; thus, the tantric writings mention 72,000 channels, and some sutras, such as *Nanda's Entry into the Womb* (*Nandagarbhāvakrāntinirdeśa*),[77] mention 80,000 channels in the human body.

With regard to the flowing energies, generally there are ten principal types: the five major and five minor energy winds.[78] The drops refer to the white element and the red element. The *Kālacakra Tantra*, however, mentions four types of drops: (1) the drop at the forehead or mid-brow that becomes manifest in the waking period; (2) the drop at the throat that becomes manifest in the dream state; (3) the drop at the heart that becomes manifest at the time of deep sleep; and (4) the drop at the navel that becomes manifest in the fourth stage (sexual climax). The *Kālacakra Tantra* gives a very detailed explanation of these; in fact, the entire structure of the body of the practitioner, that is, the channels, energies, and drops, is called the internal Kālacakra. This internal Kālacakra is the basis of purification according to the practices of that particular tantra. The *Kālacakra Tantra* speaks of three types of Kālacakra, or wheel of time: external, internal, and alternative.

On the basis of deep insight into the subtle nature of one's own body, the meditator pinpoints critical points within the body and penetrates them in meditation. As a result of this, he or she is able to dissolve and withdraw the flows and processes of the gross levels of mind and the corresponding energy winds. Eventually, the meditator is able to generate the subtlest level of clear light—that is, the clear light of death—into the entity of the path, the wisdom realizing emptiness. Gaining such a realization is like finding a key with which you can open any treasure chest. With that key, you can attain the complete enlightenment of buddhahood through the path of Guhyasamāja, actualizing the illusory body by using the methods explained in the *Guhyasamāja Tantra*; you can become enlightened through the path explained in the *Kālacakra Tantra*, by achieving the empty form;[79] or you can become enlightened through the practices of the rainbow body, as explained in *Cakrasaṃvara Tantra* or the teachings of Dzog-chen.

Once the practitioner has gained mastery over the mind and the ability to use it for practices of the path during the waking state, he or she can then use it for practices of the path during the dream state as well. These meditations are known as the *nine mixings*: three mixings during the waking state, three during the dream state, and three during death.[80]

It is said that the best practitioner of Highest Yoga Tantra is one who can attain complete enlightenment within this lifetime; the intermediate level practitioner attains complete enlightenment in the intermediate state; the inferior level practitioner attains complete enlightenment in a future life. Practitioners in the two latter categories are taught the practice of transference of consciousness.[81] There is also a similar practice called "entering into a town," which is a form of resurrection where the individual's consciousness leaves its old body and enters the body of a sentient being who has just died. All these techniques belong to a collection of meditative practices known as the *six yogas of Naropa*;[82] these are the tantric instructions that the Indian master Naropa extracted from many different tantras and are the core of the meditative tradition of the Kagyu lineage. The Gelug tradition also emphasizes the practice of the six yogas of Naropa,[83] and one also finds these meditations in the Sakya practice of Path and Fruition, or Lam-dre. Also, we can find the essential elements of this practice in the Nyingma practice known as "the heart's drop."

HIGHEST YOGA TANTRA ACCORDING TO THE
OLD TRANSLATION SCHOOL

We have just discussed the mode of procedure of Highest Yoga
Tantra according to the New Translation Schools. However, in
the Old Translation, or Nyingma, school there is reference to the
practices of the Great Perfection Vehicle—Mahātiyoga. The
teachings on the meditative practices of the Great Perfection
Vehicle consist of three categories: (1) the category of mind,
(2) the category of quintessential instructions, and (3) the category of space. Although there is substantial literature on these
topics, it is still difficult to discern the many subtleties of the
practices associated with these three categories of teachings.
Among the three, the collection of quintessential instructions is
said to be the most profound. One could say that the practice of
the other two—the categories of mind and space—lays a foundation for the practice of breakthrough, mentioned previously.

The view of emptiness as explained in the categories of mind
and space has some unique features that distinguish it from the
view of emptiness found in the other eight vehicles within the
ninefold division of yānas. However, it is quite difficult to elucidate this point. The teachings in the collection of quintessential
instructions speak of two purposes: the actualization of the
pristinely pure inner radiance dharmakāya and the actualization of
the *spontaneous outer radiance saṃbhogakāya*. According to the
explanations of some masters, one actualizes these two embodiments of an enlightened being through the breakthrough and
leap-over practices. By understanding these different elements of
the Great Perfection school, you can develop a better understanding of the great perfection of the base, the great perfection
of the path, and the great perfection of the resultant state.

As explained before, these factors can be understood only
through experience; they cannot be described through mere
words. One can begin to appreciate the profundity and difficulty

of attaining this view by reading Longchen Rabjampa's own text on the practices of the Great Perfection, *The Treasury of the Supreme Vehicle* (*Theg mchog mdzod*). The root text is very difficult, and the autocommentary is rather copious and itself difficult to comprehend. Another text by Longchenpa is *The Treasury of the Expanse of Reality* (*Chos dbyings mdzod*), in which he also outlines the practices of the Great Perfection. In fact, this second text is like the key to Dzog-chen. Only by comprehending the practices of Great Perfection based on these two texts can you hope to have a good, reliable understanding of the Great Perfection. It is also important to study Kunkhyen Jigme Lingpa's text, *Treasury of Enlightened Attributes* (*Yon tan mdzod*), at the end of which you will find an explanation of Dzog-chen practice.

You can also consult other texts composed by masters who themselves have had experiences of the Great Perfection, highly realized masters who have been able to extract the essence of the various elements of the Great Perfection practices and as a result have been able to explain them concisely and succinctly. However, if we were to try to understand the practices of Dzog-chen on the basis of these short texts alone, it would be extremely difficult. For example, the shortest wisdom sutra is said to consist of the single letter ĀḤ. This single letter captures the entire meaning of the emptiness of all phenomena. However, it is not enough for us to just repeat this letter and reflect on it alone. Although the Buddha might have been able to convey the entire essence of the doctrine of emptiness in a single letter, there is no guarantee that we can understand it fully by reliance on this alone.

As we discussed previously during our question and answer session, when we study Madhyamaka philosophy, we must study it in all its complexities, examining the different elements and reasonings by which proponents of the Madhyamaka school reach the conclusion that all phenomena lack inherent existence. In addition, to fully understand this philosophical view and all its subtle implications, we must understand the views of the lower schools of thought as well.

In one way, our final conclusion is quite simple!—because phenomena are dependent on causes and conditions and other factors as well, they lack independent status. Hence, all phenomena are devoid of inherent existence. But although this conclusion seems simple, if you try to approach the Prāsaṅgika view of emptiness directly, from the very beginning—"because things are interdependent and dependently originated, they are empty"— you probably will not understand its full implications and import. Similarly, when you read a short text on the Great Perfection, even one composed by an experienced lama, if you feel that the view and practice of Dzog-chen is quite simple, it is a sign that you have not understood it properly. It would be quite ironic if the highest of the nine vehicles, the Great Perfection, were the most simple! That would be very ironic indeed!

20

QUESTIONS AND ANSWERS

Q: YOUR HOLINESS, AS I UNDERSTAND IT, in the past advanced tantric practices were given out in a very controlled way and normally in the context of a guru-disciple relationship. Today, such practices are freely available and are even given to beginners. Why has this change occurred, and are there any dangers in this new approach?

HHDL: There are certainly some dangers in this approach, but it also has a purpose. There already exists a proliferation of tantric literature, much of which, unfortunately, misinterprets tantric practices; this is very harmful in that it generates misunderstandings about tantra. Giving teachings that explain tantra correctly will help clear up this confusion.

Although I do not claim to have high realizations or a great knowledge of tantra, I can see that there is much confusion. This has been caused by the spread of tantric teachings by certain teachers who lack knowledge and their disciples, who are themselves not properly qualified. Therefore, proper explanations of tantric practices given by qualified tantric masters can really help to clear up these misunderstandings.

Q: Your Holiness, in a commentary on the writings of Longchenpa, His Holiness Dudjom Rinpoche wrote that the nature of voidness can be directly perceived. Can you please explain how the ordinary practitioner learns to perceive voidness directly?

147

Also, if voidness can be directly perceived, why is it so difficult to realize emptiness?

HHDL: In this respect, I think it is important to first understand what is meant by emptiness, or voidness, and ultimate truth. In Buddhist writings, there are many different references to ultimate truth in texts such as Maitreya's *Madhyāntavibhāga* (*Discriminating the Middle Way from the Extremes*), in which he speaks of three different usages of the term *ultimate*: the ultimate meaning, the ultimate attainment, and the ultimate path.[84] Similarly, in his *Uttaratantra*, Maitreya speaks of ultimate and relative objects of refuge.[85] Then again, in a treatise called *Satyadvayavibhāga* (*Analysis of the Two Truths*), the Indian master Jñānagarbha speaks of two types of ultimate meaning: the actual ultimate and the concordant ultimate, or similitude of the ultimate, both of which are again explained on two different levels. Furthermore, according to tantras such as the *Guhyasamāja Tantra*, the meaning clear light is ultimate truth and the illusory body is conventional truth.

Similarly, there are different meanings of the term *emptiness*. We have already seen that the various philosophical schools of Buddhism propound differing interpretations of emptiness. Moreover, the *Kālacakra Tantra* speaks of a specific type of emptiness: the emptiness of all forms of materiality. This emptiness is, in turn, understood on two different levels: objectified emptiness and non-objectified emptiness. Then, in the tantric terminology of the *Guhyasamāja Tantra*, four types of emptiness are described. These refer to the four types of experience one has during the dissolution processes at the time of death: (1) the *empty* occurs when the gross levels of mind, that is, the eighty indicative conceptions, dissolve; (2) the *great empty* occurs when all subtle appearances dissolve; (3) the *very empty* occurs during the dissolution of red increase; and (4) the *complete empty* refers to the experience of the actual clear light, which itself is divided into *objective clear light*, which is emptiness, and *subjective clear light*. Perhaps my answer has created more confusion, but I think it is important to be aware of all of these subtleties!

The term *non-conceptuality*, likewise, takes on a variety of different meanings according to the varying contexts in which it is used. There are non-conceptual states of mind common to both Buddhist and non-Buddhist practices. Within the sutra system, there are non-conceptual states of tranquil abiding and non-conceptual states of directly realizing emptiness. There are also non-conceptual states in the Generation Stage and the Completion Stage. Even within the Completion Stage, there are the non-conceptual states of ordinary beings and those of superior beings. Thus, we find that there are many different levels and, therefore, different connotations for even this one single term, depending on the context and the level of discussion.

The Nyingma master Dodrup Jigme Tenpai Nyima has mentioned that although we may use a term such as *great wonderment* in Dzog-chen, there are many different types of great wonderment, ranging from the shock experienced by a beggar when attacked by a pack of dogs, all the way up to the great wonderment of the ultimate realization of the Completion Stage. There are so many different types of wonderment.[86]

You can now see that to pick and try to understand one word, such as *emptiness*, is not very easy. We must know all the various meanings in different contexts and the way to practice them. In the end, you may come to realize the special meaning of the Dzog-chen viewpoint. Generally, in the practice of Highest Yoga Tantra and especially in the meditative techniques of Dzog-chen, more emphasis is placed on the subjective experience of emptiness than on objective emptiness.

In Dzog-chen, the entire practice is based on three faculties: entity (or purity), nature (or spontaneity), and compassion. Thus, the entity, which is purity, is objective emptiness as expounded by the Buddha in the second turning of the wheel. Without an understanding of emptiness as taught in the wisdom sutras, no significant progress in the Dzog-chen practices of breakthrough and leap-over can take place.

With a proper understanding of the practices of the Great Perfection school, you can employ those meditative techniques that do not depend upon the dissolution of the grosser levels of mind and in which you will be able to contemplate and reflect upon the clear light nature of your own mind. Although you might have conscious experiences of the delusions, since they too are part of consciousness, they also have the nature of luminosity and knowing. Just as a sesame seed is pervaded by oil, in the same way, all mental factors, whether negative or positive, are pervaded by a luminous and cognizing fundamental nature If you understand the techniques of Dzog-chen properly, you will be able to remain aware of that basic nature of mind even when you experience the gross levels of the delusions. This technique is unique to Dzog-chen meditation.

Longchen Rabjampa has said in his writings[87] that although he could see many people practicing Great Perfection, in many cases what they were actually practicing was mere nothingness. Therefore, this is a profound and difficult practice. And since it is an exceedingly difficult path, it is not something that can be studied or taught through words alone. Instead, the practitioner, having accumulated an excellent foundation in the form of a vast collection of merit, should seek to understand it through the expert guidance of an experienced master. If these factors are complete, one will be able to derive the greatest benefit from the methods of the Great Perfection.

Q: I have taken some initiations but seem able to practice only Chenrezig. Would it be best for me not to take the Tārā initiation?

HHDL: You can either take the Tārā initiation or leave it. It would not make much difference in terms of the volume of your practice requirements. Since you have received the initiation of Chenrezig and have already taken the basic tantric commitments, taking the Tārā initiation will not involve anything extra. Also, there is no rift between Chenrezig and Tārā!

Q: In relation to the nature of mind, what is luminosity?

HHDL: In this context, it might be interesting to reflect on a passage from the Sakya literature, which says that between the arising of different moments of conceptual thought, the clear light nature of mind occurs uninterruptedly.[88]

Let us say that you look at an object that is not especially colorful, but whose color is instead somewhat muted and unattractive. Gaze at it intently for awhile. While looking at this dull-colored object, make a strong determination to maintain your concentration and focus your attention on your own perception and experience, without allowing yourself to be distracted by other external or internal objects. In the context of this level of mindfulness, you will be able to observe the exact moment your mind becomes distracted. If you hear, for example, a melodious tune, the moment you are distracted, you will realize it immediately and will then reinforce your mindfulness by withdrawing from the distraction. If memories of past experiences arise, or if thoughts of the future come up, you will also immediately recognize your distraction. Generally, various conceptual thoughts are constantly arising in our minds, moment by moment, and function to obscure its essential nature. When you utilize this technique of mindfulness and maintain your awareness on only the object in front of you, immediately perceiving the distractions and withdrawing from them, eventually you will clear away all the conceptual events that obscure the natural state of your mind. You will gradually perceive a very stable and lucid state of mind.

Ordinarily, our mind is heavily obscured by concepts and

different states of thought and emotion. In order to recognize and identify the essential nature of the mind, it is necessary to peel away the different conceptual layers and clear the obscurations. In this way, we will be able to see the true face of our own mind. This is the technique by which one seeks the object of meditation, the essential mind itself, in order to develop calm abiding focused on it.

If you apply yourself to these practices and experiments and gain your own experiences, then when you speak about consciousness in the future, you will no longer be speaking mere words. Your experience will enable you to understand what "consciousness" implies and what it is. Consciousness is a non-obstructing phenomenon, is non-material, and has the quality of luminosity, that is, it reflects any object by arising in the aspect of that object.

Consciousness is like a crystal stone; while a crystal is resting on a colored surface, you cannot see the real untinted clarity of the crystal stone, but once you take the crystal away from the colored surface, you can perceive its actual clarity.

Luminosity, or the natural clarity of the mind, is something that I cannot fully explain to you in words. If, on the other hand, you undertake these experiments on your own, you will begin to understand through experience and will eventually be able to say, "Ah! *That* is the luminous nature of mind!"

Q: Your Holiness, could you please say some more about guru yoga as practiced in the main Tibetan traditions? It seems to be an important subject that you have touched on only lightly at this time. Also, I wonder if you think that a complete study of all the explanations of the tantras and Dzog-chen is necessary in all cases, seeing that time is so short.

HHDL: This is very true—time is very short! Normally, when I teach the *Great Exposition of Tantra* (*sNgags rim chen mo*) of Tsongkhapa, it usually takes at least twenty days, even without

152

interruption for the translation. Here, we finished an entire overview of Tibetan Buddhism in just over nine hours, and most of that time was taken up by my interpreter!

Guru yoga practice is very important and should only be undertaken when you have, from the depth of your heart, taken someone as your root guru. On the basis of seeing that person as your root guru, you can practice the guru yoga of the inseparability of the deity and your guru.

In the *Gurupañcāśikā*, a text that outlines the appropriate manner of relating to one's guru in the context of Highest Yoga Tantra, it is stated that if you are unable to follow any advice given by your guru, you should explain this to your guru directly. This way of relating is very much in accordance with the general procedure of the Buddhist path. In the sutras, the Buddha himself explains that any advice given by one's guru should be followed if it accords with virtuous practice. If, however, it is counter to virtuous practice, even though it is the advice of one's guru, it should definitely not be followed. In the Vinaya teachings as well, he states that if one's guru gives advice that is contradictory to the Dharma, then you should respond and explain that it is wrong. If students sincerely point out the faults of the guru and explain any contradictory behavior, this will, in fact, help the guru to correct that behavior and adjust any wrong actions. This is the reason I am explaining this.

I apply the same principles to myself. I always emphasize to Tibetans and others that if there is anything in my teachings that you find beneficial and useful then you should implement that in your life; if there are things that are not useful or beneficial, then just leave them aside.

With regard to guru yoga, it is also important to differentiate between the definitive guru and the interpretative guru. The definitive guru is the most subtle clear light mind of the practitioner. Thus, it is possible to view one's own mind, the guru, and the meditational deity as indivisible. Otherwise, when we think of these three as inseparable, we have a vision of three people tied together with a rope!

Q: Could Your Holiness please explain the meaning of blessings, how they are given and how they are received?

HHDL: In Tibetan, the word for blessing is *jin-lab*. This means transformation through majesty or power. In short, the meaning of blessing is to bring about, as a result of the experience, a transformation in one's mind for the better. Buddhist scriptures also speak of consecrating, or blessing, a site, for instance, the site for a mandala. In that context, I am not so sure of the exact meaning of the word.

Q: There are two kinds of initiation: in Tibetan, *je-nang* and *wang*. Of these, only a limited je-nang can be given to a public audience. Many people present today are non-Buddhists, and even the Buddhists present will not receive a wang. Would Your Holiness please explain the value of today's initiation?

HHDL: Among the audience at an initiation, there will be some who are not yet prepared to take the commitments of a full initiation and others who may not wish to take the initiation at all. Therefore, I usually suggest to these people not to perform the visualizations, which are integral parts of an initiation ceremony. A je-nang, or permission, is given only to a person who has previously received an empowerment or initiation. The initiation of Tārā, which will be conducted at this time, contains all the four initiations condensed into a blessing of Tārā. Therefore, the prerequisite on the part of the recipient is to have previously received an initiation of any Highest Yoga Tantra deity.

Q: What is the solution to a religious war, where both parties claim divine right to some land?

HHDL: Perhaps the solution is to aggravate the conflict more and more! When people get so caught up in a situation that no one has the wish to listen, then no one has any common sense. Perhaps there is no alternative at that point but to fight, fight, fight, until one day both sides become exhausted!

Q: For the benefit of the uninitiated, would Your Holiness please explain what daily practices should be performed, what motivations are appropriate, and what benefits result from them in order that we may benefit fully from the Tārā initiation?

HHDL: As soon as you wake up in the morning, if you have any interest in spiritual development, you should examine your own mind and try to develop some kind of proper motivation. Then, make a strong pledge, or determination, that in the future, and especially on this day, you will practice proper behavior and proper ways of thinking. Think that you will help others in the proper ways, and if that is not possible, at least you will refrain from harming them. Then, from time to time during the day, constantly remind yourself of that determination, that motivation.

In the late evening, look back on the day to see if you really spent your day as you pledged in the morning. If you find something positive, then good—feel happy! Reinforce that determination by rejoicing in your own good actions and by resolving to continue such activities in the future. If you find you have done something negative during the day, you should feel remorse for those wrong actions committed and chastise yourself, reflecting on how these same negative actions, committed in the past, are the reason why you are still experiencing undesirable consequences. Think that if you continue to indulge in such actions in the future, this will lead you into similar undesirable consequences again.

This is the way: try, try, try! Then, over time, there is hope.

There is the possibility to improve oneself. Blessings from others are not sufficient. As a Buddhist, there are thousands and thousands, millions and billions of buddhas and bodhisattvas out there; but we are here, still passing through many difficulties every time something goes wrong. So blessings are not enough. Is that clear? Blessings must come from within. Without your own effort, it is impossible for blessings to come. Do you agree?

Translator's Notes

Part I

1. For example, the *Descent into Laṅkā Sutra* (*Laṅkāvatāra-sūtra*), one of the most important sutras of the Mahayana school of Buddhism, mentions some of these various systems. For an English translation, see D. T. Suzuki's *The Lankavatara Sutra*.

2. For a detailed discussion on the form and formless realms and the corresponding meditative states that lead to birth in these realms, see Lati Rinpoche et al., *Meditative States in Tibetan Buddhism*. The principal Indian sources for topics relating to various meditative states associated with the form and formless realms are *Abhidharmasamuccaya* and *Śrāvakabhūmi*, both by Asaṅga, and Vasubandhu's *Abhidharmakośa*.

3. For a brief description of the attitude of bodhicitta, see p. 24. For a more extensive treatment, refer to discussion on *lo-jong* and the bodhisattva's training as presented in chapter 9.

4. As is the case among contemporary scholars, there is a divergence of views within the Tibetan scholastic tradition as to the exact date of the Buddha's birth. There are two especially well-known positions, that of Atīśa (the Indian master who came to Tibet in the eleventh century), and that of Sakya Paṇḍita Kunga Gyaltsen (1182–1251). The former's position does not differ much from that of the Kashmiri Pandit Śākya Śrī, which, as mentioned by His Holiness, accords well with the standard position of the Theravāda tradition. According to this

view, the birth of Siddhārtha Gautama (as he was known prior to his enlightenment) was 623 B.C.E., and the death, 543 B.C.E. According to modern Western scholarship the dates should be 563 B.C.E. and 483 B.C.E., respectively, that is to say, a good sixty years later. However, according to Sakya Paṇḍita's calculation, the Buddha was born more than 3,000 years ago.

5. Sarnath is located near Benares (modern day Varanasi) in Uttar Pradesh.

6. It should be mentioned that the various turnings of the wheel of Dharma do not, in general, refer to individual discourses given on particular occasions. Rather, they provide a framework for categorizing the Buddha's teachings according to subject matter and the philosophical view employed. This hermeneutical method of distinguishing between different "turnings," seen only in the Mahayana traditions, is very complex and the subject of some controversy. In brief, we can say that the Buddha's first discourse at Deer Park set in motion, or commenced, the (mode of teaching that became known as the) first turning of the wheel of Dharma.

7. The three higher trainings, described more fully in the next section, are the trainings in ethics, concentration, and wisdom. These three trainings are called "higher trainings" only when they are conjoined with renunciation, the genuine intention to become free from samsara—the perpetual cycle of dissatisfactory conditioned existence.

8. The Three Jewels of Buddhism are (1) the Buddha-Jewel, the enlightened teacher, or one's own future state of enlightenment; (2) the Dharma-Jewel, the teachings and realizations that lead to happiness, liberation, and enlightenment; and (3) the Sangha-Jewel, the spiritual community of those well established on the Buddhist path.

9.   All eighteen sub-schools of Vaibhāṣika stem from two original schools: Mahāsaṁgikas and Sthāviras. For a summary of the alternative presentations of this division into eighteen, see Jeffrey Hopkins' *Meditation on Emptiness*, pp. 713–19. It should be noted that Bhāvaviveka mentions three different views regarding the manner of division in his *Tarkajvālā*; these are cited by Changkya Rolpai Dorje in his *Presentation of Philosophical Systems: The Ornament Beautifying the Buddha's Doctrine*, pp. 73–75.

10.   Absorptive meditation encompasses many different meditative states, such as the absorptions of the form and formless states. The form state absorptions are differentiated on the basis of their different branches as well as the factors that characterize them, whereas the formless state absorptions are differentiated according to their particular object of absorption. In the latter case, the subtler the object, the more advanced the state of absorption. For a concise exposition on the differentiation between the four form states and the four formless states, see Lati Rinpoche et al., *Meditative States in Tibetan Buddhism*, pp. 128–33.

11.   In his *Abhidharmakoṣa*, chapter 6, verse 15, Vasubandhu states that meditation on the mindfulnesses of body, feelings, mind, and phenomena constitute meditative contemplation on the four characteristics of conditioned existence (which are explained in relation to the First Noble Truth). These are impermanence, suffering (*duḥkha*), emptiness, and selflessness. In particular, each respective mindfulness contemplation is associated with the elimination of the particular misapprehensions that contradict our correct ascertainment of each of these four characteristics. Contemplation of the impure nature of one's bodily substances eliminates the misapprehension of the body as clean and desirable; mindfulness of the unsatisfactory nature of feelings counters the attachment to pleasurable feelings; mindfulness of the momentary nature of mind counteracts the apprehension of an

enduring "self"; and the mindful contemplation of phenomena counteracts the apprehension of phenomena as possessing self-evident identities. However, Maitreya relates the four mindfulnesses to each of the Four Noble Truths in his *Madhyāntavibhāga*, chapter 4, verse 1. The reason why body, feelings, mind, and phenomena are specifically chosen for deep contemplation is that they are the principal objects that form the basis for our grasping at "self" and the delusory states that arise from this ignorance. A concise exposition of the four mindfulnesses based on the above two Indian treatises can be found in the second part of Tsongkhapa's *Golden Rosary of True Eloquence: An Extensive Exposition of the Abhisamayālaṃkāra and its Commentary*, volume *tsha* (18), folios 19b–21a.

12. Vultures' Peak is popularly identified with a hilly site in Rajghir in modern India's Bihar State.

13. Most of the *Perfection of Wisdom* sutras have been translated into English by Edward Conze. See bibliography.

14. For further discussion on the four reliances, see Robert Thurman's translation, *The Central Philosophy of Tibet: A Study and Translation of Jey Tsong Khapa's Essence of True Eloquence,* pp. 113–30; also Hopkins, *Meditation on Emptiness,* p. 425.

15. This is one of the most frequently quoted verses attributed to the Buddha. To my knowledge, no source sutra for the verse has been found in the the Tibetan translation of the Buddha's words, or *Kangyur* (*bKa' 'gyur*). Tibetan commentators cite it from *Vimalaprabhā,* Kulika Puṇḍarīka's famous commentary on the *Kālacakra Tantra.* However, Thurman asserts that the verse can be found in the Pali canon and also that a Sanskrit version appears in D. Shastri's edition of the *Tattvasaṃgraha.* See Thurman's *The Central Philosophy of Tibet,* p. 190, footnote 12.

16. The collection of hymns include: (1) *Nirupamastava*, (2) *Dharmadhātustotra*, (3) *Acintyastava*, (4) *Cittavajrastava*, (5) *Lokātitastava*, (6) *Kāyatrayastotra*, and (7) *Stutyatitastava*.

17. There are three English translations of this important work: E. Obermiller's *Sublime Science of the Great Vehicle to Salvation*; J. Takasaki's, *A Study on the Ratnagotravibhāga*; and *The Changeless Nature*, translated from the Tibetan by Ken and Katia Holmes.

18. An elaborate discussion on the three natures based on the *Sutra Unravelling the Thought of the Buddha* can be found in Tsongkhapa's *Essence of True Eloquence*. For an English translation of the relevant sections of Tsongkhapa's work, see Thurman's *The Central Philosophy of Tibet*, especially pp. 191–203.

19. The translation given here is based on Herbert Guenther's translation from the Tibetan version in his *Life and Teachings of Naropa*, p. 120, with slight modification.

20. See Part 3, especially the chapter on Highest Yoga Tantra.

21. *Madhyamakāvatāra*, chapter 6, verse 131. For an English translation, see C. W. Huntington, Jr., *The Emptiness of Emptiness*, p. 173.

22. The twelve links (in the chain) of dependent orgination are: ignorance, action, consciousness, name and form, sources, contact, feelings, attachment, grasping, becoming, birth, and aging and death. For an extensive discussion on the twelve links, see the Dalai Lama's *The Meaning of Life from a Buddhist Perspective*, especially chapters 1 and 2; see also Pabongka Rinpoche's *Liberation in the Palm of Your Hand*, pp. 506–34.

23. Chapter 3, verse 28b.

24. *Guhyasamāja Tantra*, chapter 7.

25. *Rice Seedling Sutra* (*Śālistambhasūtra*), p. 303.

26. For an English translation, see Edward Conze's *Perfect Wisdom: The Short Prajñāpāramitā Texts*.

27. For an informative discussion on the origin of the Jonangpa school (the principal school advocating the Shen-tong view) and a concise introduction to the disputes among Tibetan scholars concerning the Shen-tong view, see Paul Williams' *Mahāyāna Buddhism*, pp. 96–109. Thuken Chökyi Nyima, in his *Crystal Mirror of Philosophical Systems*, pp. 218–9, lists nine sutras as being cited by the proponents of Shen-tong as their primary source sutras. Among these are *Tathāgatagarbhasūtra*, *Jñānālokālaṃkārasūtra*, *Śrīmālādevīsiṁhanāda*, *Mahāparinirvāṇasūtra*, *Avataṁsakasūtra*, *Ratnakūtasūtra*, *Mahābherīhārakaparivartasūtra*, *Suvarṇaprabhāsasūtra* and *'Phel ba dang 'grib pa med par bstan pa'i mdo*.

28. Some of the synonyms used in the wisdom sutras are *ultimate emptiness, emptiness of nature, emptiness of that which is beyond extremes,* and so forth. These synonyms can be found in the Mahayana scriptures where emptiness is presented in various divisions, e.g., as four, sixteen, eighteen, and twenty emptinesses. For a discussion on these divisions, see *Madhyamakāvatāra*, chapter 6, verses 179–223; see C. W. Huntington, Jr., pp. 179–183 for an English translation of the section. See also Geshe Rabten's *Echoes of Voidness*, pp. 85–91.

29. This refers to a particular system of classification of all existent reality that is found in the perfection of wisdom literature. The list begins with the five aggregates, the first of which is

form, and ends with *omniscience.* Hence the expression "from form up to omniscience" is equivalent to "all phenomena" or "all things and events."

30. *Mūlamadhyamakakārikā,* chapter 24, verse 19; for an English translation, see F. Streng's *Emptiness: A Study in Religious Meaning,* p. 213.

31. *Mūlamadhyamakakārikā,* chapter 24, verse 14; Streng, p. 213.

32. A partial translation of Candrakīrti's *Prasannapadā* can be found in M. Sprung's *Lucid Exposition of the Middle Way.*

33. One of the earliest presentations of this fourfold analysis is found in the *Sutra Unravelling the Thought of the Buddha,* one of the most important hermeneutical scriptures in Mahayana Buddhism. A clearer exposition of these principles, based on the abovementioned sutra, can be found in Asaṅga's *Abhidharmasamuccaya* and its related commentaries. For a contemporary discussion on the topic, see Matthew Kapstein's "Mipham's Theory of Interpretation" in *Buddhist Hermeneutics,* Donald Lopez, Jr., ed., pp. 152–61.

34. See Tsongkhapa's *Great Exposition of the Stages of Path,* volume *pa* (13), folio 405a.

35. Verse 12.

PART II

36. An English translation of this important Mahayana work can be found in *A Guide to the Bodhisattva's Way of Life* by Stephen Batchelor. There is also an earlier translation from the original

Sanskrit by Marion L. Matics under the name *Entering the Path to Enlightenment*. Finally, a more recent bilingual edition with the Sanskrit and English, translated by Parmananda Sharma was published by Aditya Prakashan, New Delhi, in 1990. For contemporary commentaries on the text, see His Holiness's works: *A Flash of Lightning in the Dark of Night*, Shambhala Publications, 1994 and *Transcendent Wisdom*, Snow Lion, 1988.

37. Chapter 4, verses 28 and 29. All quotations from the *Bodhicaryāvatāra* given here are based on Stephen Batchelor's translation, with slight modifications where necessary.

38. Chapter 4, verses 30 and 31.

39. Chapter 4, verse 33.

40. Chapter 4, verse 46.

41. Chapter 6, verse 7.

42. Chapter 6, verse 39.

43. There exists a partial English translation of this work from the Sanskrit original by Giuseppe Tucci, 1934 and 1936. However, a full English translation of the *Ratnāvali* from the Tibetan edition by Lati Rinpoche and Jeffrey Hopkins can be found as "The Precious Garland of Advice for the King" in *The Buddhism of Tibet* by the Dalai Lama, et al.

44. For an extensive discussion on this practice, see the Dalai Lama's *Path to Bliss*, pp. 61–74.

PART III

45. Regarding the historical juncture in which the tantric teachings in general—and the *Kālacakra Tantra* in particular—evolved, there are differing opinions among traditional Tibetan scholars. One school of thought maintains that tantric teachings were first given by the Buddha on a full moon day one year after his full enlightenment. A second view maintains that tantric teachings were given by the Buddha one month prior to his *parinirvāṇa*. In his lectures, His Holiness suggested that this second view seems to be more consistent, since the *Root Tantra of Kālacakra* (*Śrīkālacakranāmatantrarāja*) itself states:

> Just as the mode of the Perfection of Wisdom
> [Was taught] by the Teacher at Vultures' Peak,
> So was taught at Śrī Dhānyakaṭaka,
> The way of the Secret Mantra.

(This verse is quoted by Butön in his *History of Kālacakra*, volume *nga* (4), folio 12b. George Roerich, in his translation of Gö Lotsawa Shönu Pal's *The Blue Annals*, identifies Dhānyakaṭaka as Amarāvatī in the Sattenpalle Taluk of Guntur district, which is now in the state of Andra Pradesh, in southern India. See *The Blue Annals*, p. 754, footnote 1.)

Of the two positions listed here on the historical evolution of the tantra, the second seems to be favored among the majority of traditional Tibetan scholars. However, in his *History of Kālacakra* (folio 13a), Butön categorically refutes it. For additional information on this issue and also on the spread of the practice of Kālacakra in Tibet, see the Dalai Lama and Jeffrey Hopkins, *Kālachakra Tantra, Rite of Initiation*, chapter 5, pp. 59–65.

46. An example of the first of these three methods is found in the *Guhyasamāja Tantra,* where the main meditative technique used in the practice of bringing about the experience of subtle clear light is prāṇayoga. This refers to a specific set of practices that essentially involve the skilful utilization of the *prāṇas* (vital energies or "winds") at critical points within the central channel. The practices of the *Cakrasaṃvara Tantra* are classic examples of the second type of method; there, the main emphasis is on the generation of the four types of bliss. In fact, this seems to be a special feature of most of the Mother Tantras. The third method refers particularly to the meditative practice of Dzog-chen in which the main emphasis seems to be on cultivating the state of non-conceptuality. I remember once His Holiness stating at a public teaching in Dharamsala, India, that he bases this observation—that there are these three distinct approaches in the Highest Yoga Tantra—on various comments found in the writings of the Gelug masters Khedup Norsang Gyatso (1423–1513) and Changkya Rolpai Dorje (1717–1786).

47. In the Tibetan tantric literature, there are various texts associated with three principal aspects of Guhyasamāja. These three aspects are: Akṣobhya Guhyasamāja of the Ārya school, Mañjuśrīvajra of the Jñānapāda school, and Lokiteśvara Guhyasamāja, which was subsumed under both schools. A detailed account of these three lineages can be found in Tsongkhapa's *Lamp Brilliantly Illuminating the Five Stages,* volume *ja* (7), folio 21b. Among these, the practices relating to Akṣobhya Guhyasamāja of the Ārya school are most predominant in the Tibetan tradition.

48. Here the term *bodhicitta* refers to a subtle physiological substance that, according to tantra, is found throughout the body. The term applies to a wide range of elements including the regen-

erative fluids of both male and female. When "melted," this essential substance can travel through the psychic channels and gather together at certain vital points within the body. Because of this, the tantric experience of bliss is intimately associated with the flow and "melting" of this essential substance. In contrast, in the sutra system *bodhicitta* refers to the mind of enlightenment, that is, the mind that genuinely aspires to attain full enlightenment for the benefit of all beings.

49. For an extensive discussion of the ninefold division of vehicles, see Dudjom Rinpoche, *The Nyingma School of Tibetan Buddhism*, volume 1, book 1.

50. Strictly speaking, the material used for this type of mandala is pulverized quartz stones, which are then dyed according to a traditional dyeing method. The Kālacakra empowerment is a typical case where this type of mandala is created for the ceremony. For a description of the Kālacakra mandala and the symbolism of its various parts, see the Dalai Lama and Jeffrey Hopkins, *The Kālachakra Tantra*, chapter 6, pp. 67–91. The Tibetan term *kyil-khor* has a connotation of wholeness or roundness, whereas the Sanskrit word *maṇḍala* suggests extracting the essence. However, in the context of the sādhana practice of a tantric meditational deity (which is the case in point here) the term refers to a cosmic symbol of the universe. Although the term is used in referring to the created artwork, the true mandala is the visualized image of the celestial residence of the meditational deity, which has been generated in your meditation. Such a residence is generated from within the sphere of emptiness and is ultimately the essence of the divine wisdom of the meditational deity itself. That divine wisdom, in turn, is inseparable from the most subtle clear light mind of the practitioner. Hence there is no subject-object duality.

51. See p. 19 for a concise definition of prātimokṣa.

52. Kongtrul Yönten Gyatso, in his *Treasury of Encyclopedic Knowledge*, vol. 2, p. 11, also cites a verse from the *Kālacakra Root Tantra* stating the same point. However, in spite of my efforts I have not been able to locate the verse in the Tibetan version of the root tantra.

53. See the Dalai Lama, *Path to Bliss*, p. 181.

54. *Gurupañcāśikā*, verse 7. See bibliographical entry under Aśvaghoṣa.

55. P5255, vol. 96, p. 416.

56. The descriptions of the five meats and the five nectars can be found in the sādhanas of the meditational deities belonging to Highest Yoga Tantra. I have not listed them here due to considerations related to certain tantric precepts.

57. For example, see Vasubandhu's *Abhidharmakośa*, chapter 4, verse 109.

58. See pp. 121 and 123 . For further discussion on the specific meaning of these technical terms from Action and Performance Tantras and their corresponding meditative states, see the Dalai Lama's "Heart of Mantra" and a passage from Tsongkhapa's *Great Exposition of Secret Mantra* in *The Yoga of Tibet*, Jeffrey Hopkins, trans., pp. 19–42 and pp. 155–71, respectively.

59. Chapter 8, verse 16.

60. See *The Yoga of Tibet*, Jeffrey Hopkins, trans., for pho-

tographs of some of the principal symbolic hand gestures, or mudrās, performed in relation to the rituals of Action and Performance Tantras.

61. *Sādhana* (literally, "means of attainment") refers to a meditation manual that outlines key elements of a deity yoga practice. In most cases, it refers to texts that describe the procedure for the meditator's full generation into the appropriate deity. A sādhana consists of the following key elements: preliminary practices, such as prayers invoking inspiration from the lineage masters of the particular tantra; some form of dissolution into emptiness; emergence as the deity from within the empty sphere, which includes also the visualization of the mandala; specific meditation on cultivating divine pride (exalted identity) and perception of the meditational deity; mantra repetition; and concluding practices.

62. *Means of Attainment Entitled "All Goodness"* (*Samantabhadranāmasādhana*).

63. See p. 125.

64. For a different enumeration, see Lati Rinpoche and Jeffrey Hopkins, *Death, Intermediate State and Rebirth in Tibetan Buddhism,* p. 30.

65. The kāyas, or embodiments of an enlightened being, are variously enumerated according to context. For example, there are divisions into two kāyas (Truth Body and Form Body), three kāyas (Truth Body, Complete Enjoyment Body, and Emanation Body), and four kāyas (Nature Body, Wisdom[-Truth] Body, Complete Enjoyment Body, and Emanation Body). In tantra, we also find enumeration in terms of five kāyas. In this case, a fifth kāya called the *Co-emergent Body* is added to the original list of four. This is according to the system of enumeration found in the tantra

called *Perfect Expression of Manjusri's Name.* There are, however, several different systems of enumerating the five kāyas in tantra.

66. "The defilements are adventitious, and the positive qualities naturally inhere." From *Uttaratantra,* chapter 1, verse 51.

67. "Abiding in the meditation on illusion, [I perceive] everything alike." Quoted in Tsongkhapa's *Lamp Brilliantly Illuminating the Five Stages,* volume *ja* (7), folio 210b.

68. Dudjom Rinpoche describes breakthrough as one of the two principal paths for full realization of pristine awareness, the other being leap-over. He defines them, stating, "...*breakthrough* (*khregs chod*), which is oriented towards the emptiness aspect or primordially pure awareness without conceptual elaboration, and so causes the cessation of empty phenomena; and *leap-over* (*thod rgal*), which clarifies the apparitional aspect or corporeal objects into inner radiance in a spontaneously present manner, and so causes the cessation of apparitional reality." See *The Nyingma School of Tibetan Buddhism,* vol. 1, pp. 334–45. The translation given here is based on that of Gyurme Dorje, with slight modification of some of the terms.

69. As His Holiness mentions below (p. 131), the main explanatory tantra that outlines these interpretive keys is *Wisdom Vajra Compendium.* A detailed commentary on this important hermeneutical text can be found in Tsongkhapa's *Exposition of Wisdom Vajra Compendium,* volume *ca* (5). For a contemporary discussion of hermeneutical methods based on this tantra and Tsongkhapa's commentary, see Robert Thurman's "Vajra Hermeneutics" in *Buddhist Hermeneutics,* Donald Lopez, Jr., ed., pp. 119–48.

70. For detailed discussion of these three stages and the dissolu-

tion process in general, see *Death, Intermediate State and Rebirth*, pp. 32–45.

71. *Pradīpoddyotananāmaṭīkā*, chapter 1, opening verse. At this point in his lecture, His Holiness mentioned that due to Candrakīrti's renown, there was once a popular saying: "Just as in the sky there are the sun and moon, on the earth there are the 'two clear (ones).'" These "two clear (ones)" are Candrakīrti's texts: *Pradīpoddyotananāmaṭīkā* and *Prasannapadā*, a commentary on Nāgārjuna's *Mūlamadhyamakakārikā*. The Tibetan titles for these two texts both contain the word *gsal*, meaning "clear" or "radiant."

72. *Pradīpoddyotana*, chapter 1, verses 2–4. The five stages as enumerated by Candrakīrti in this passage are (1) Generation Stage, (2) isolation of mind, (3) illusory body, (4) clear light, and (5) union. Their corresponding initiations are (1) vase initiation, (2) secret initiation (for stages 2 and 3), (3) wisdom-knowledge initiation (for stage 4), and (4) word initiation (for stage 5).

73. An example of a sādhana that uses this division into causal and resultant vajra holders is the solitary aspect of Yamāntaka Vajrabhairava. *Vajra holder* is a technical name referring to the perfect embodied form that arises in the meditative state of a tantric sādhana. In other tantras, it is referred to as Vajradhara.

74. This refers to five principal stages in the general procedure of generating into the meditational deity: (1) clarification through suchness, (2) clarification through moon, (3) clarification through seed [syllable], (4) clarification through symbol, and (5) clarification through full emergence into the exalted body.

75. For a systematic account on the various levels of the Generation Stage of Highest Yoga Tantra, see Ngawang Palden's

presentation as translated by Daniel Cozort in *Highest Yoga Tantra*, pp. 48–52.

76. These are cakras at the crown, throat, heart, navel, and secret region. For a detailed description of the three principal channels and the channel centers, see Geshe Kelsang Gyatso's *Clear Light of Bliss*, pp. 17–24.

77. P760.13, volume 23, p. 97.

78. The five major, or root, winds are: the life-supporting, the downward-voiding, the upward-moving, the equally-abiding, and the pervading wind. The five minor winds are: the moving, the intensely moving, the perfectly moving, the strongly moving, and the definitely moving wind. For their descriptions, colors, locations, and specific functions, see Geshe Kelsang Gyatso's *Clear Light of Bliss*, pp. 24–32.

79. This refers to a meditative technique unique to the *Kālacakra Tantra*, in which the practitioner's physical body de-materializes. The term "empty form" indicates refining the body to such a stage that its nature transcends corporeality. There is a concise but informative discussion of this specific practice in Ngawang Palden's *Presentation of the Grounds and Paths of the Four Great Secret Tantra Classes*. See Daniel Cozort, *Highest Yoga Tantra*, pp. 121–131.

80. For detailed discussion on the nine mixings, see Geshe Kelsang Gyatso's *Clear Light of Bliss*, pp. 100–121.

81. A short description of this practice can be found in Garma C. C. Chang's *Teachings of Tibetan Yoga*, pp. 111–15.

82. The six yogas are: inner heat, illusory body, dream yoga, clear

light, intermediate state, and transference. Another system of enumeration lists resurrection in place of the yoga of the intermediate state.

83. Tsongkhapa, the founder of the Gelug tradition, has written an extensive commentary on the six yogas, entitled *A Commentary on the Profound Path of the Six Yogas of Naropa Endowed with Three Convictions*, volume *ta* (9) of his *Collected Works*.

84. Chapter 3, verse 11.

85. Chapter 1, verses 20, 21.

86. Dodrup Jigme Tenpai Nyima, *Miscellaneous Works on Great Perfection*, p. 203 in the *Collected Works*, vol. *ca* (5).

87. This is probably a reference to Longchenpa's *Treasury of the Expanse of Reality*.

88. This statement is generally attributed to Sakya Paṇḍita Kunga Gyaltsen.

GLOSSARY

ADETAILED EXPLANATION of many of the technical terms and their defini-
tions along with various possible English translations can be found in
the "Glossary of Key Tibetan, Buddhist and Sanskrit Terms" by Geshe
Thupten Jinpa and Dr. Gyurme Dorje in *A Handbook of Tibetan Culture*,
Graham Coleman (ed.), London: Random House, 1993.

English	Tibetan	Sanskrit
Action Tantra	bya rgyud	kriyātantra
all-encompassing (or con-	'dus pa rdor dbang	
densed) vajra initiation		
all-pervading vajra space	mkha' khyab mkha'i	
	rdo rje can	
appearance of all	kun snang gi ting	
	nge 'dzin	
beneficial empowerment	phan pa'i dbang	
blessing	byin rlabs	
bodhicitta	byang chub kyi sems	bodhicitta
Bodhisattva Vehicle	byang sems kyi theg pa	bodhisattvayana
Brahma Vehicle	tshang pa'i theg pa	brahmayāna
breakthrough	khregs chod	
Buddha's Vehicle	sangs rgyas kyi theg pa	buddhayāna
category of mind	sems sde	
category of quintessential instructions	man ngag gi sde	
category of space	klong sde	
causal meditative stabilization	rgyu'i ting nge 'dzin	
causal tantra	rgyu'i rgyud	
causal vajra holder	rgyu rdo rje 'dzin pa	
compassion	thugs rje	karuṇā
Chenrezig	sPyan ras gzigs	Avalokiteśvara
Complete Enjoyment Body	long spyod rdzogs pa'i sku	saṃbhogakāya

English	Tibetan	Sanskrit
complete empty	thams cad stong pa	sarvaśūnya
Completion Stage	rdzogs rim	
concentration abiding in fire	me gnas kyi bsam gtan	
concentration abiding in sound	sgra gnas kyi bsam gtan	
concentration which bestows liberation at the end of sound	sgra mthar thar pa ster ba'i bsam gtan	
conditioned existence	'khor ba	saṃsāra
consciousness	rnam par shes pa	vijñāna
constant co-cognition	lhan cig dmigs nges	sahopalambhaniyama
contaminated phenomena	zag bcas kyi chos	
definitive	nges don	nīthārtha
deity of emptiness	stong pa'i lha	
deity of letter	yi ge'i lha	
deity of seal	phyag rgya'i lha	
deity of sound	gra'i lha	
deity of the symbol	phyag mtshan gyi lha	
deity yoga	lha'i rnal 'byor	
dependent phenomena	gzhan dbang gyi chos	paratantra
devoid of intrinsic reality and identity	rang bzhin gyis grub pa'i ngo bo med pa	
dhyāni buddha	gshegs pa	
dhyāni consort	gshegs ma	
direct perception	mngon sum	pratyakṣa
discipline; monastic rule	'dul ba	Vinaya
discipline of individual liberation	so sor thar pa	prātimokṣa
divine pride	lha'i nga rgyal	
eightfold noble path	'phags lam yan lag brgyad	
Emanation Body	sprul sku	nirmāṇakāya
embodiments of an enlightened being	sans rgyas kyi sku	kāya
empowerment	dbang	abhiṣeka
emptiness	stong pa nyid	śūnyatā
"Emptiness of other" school (Shen-tong)	gzhan stong	
empty	stong pa	śūnya
empty form	stong gzugs	śūnyarūpa
entity/being	ngo bo	svabhāva
equalizing (and exchanging) oneself and others	bdag gzhan mnyam brjes	

English	Tibetan	Sanskrit
Father Tantra	pha rgyud	
female lay practitioner	dge bsnyen ma	upāsikā
five clarifications	mngon byang lnga	
Form Body	gzugs sku	rūpakāya
form deity	gzugs kyi lha	
form realm	gzugs khams	rūpadhātu
formless realm	gzugs med khams	ārūpyadhātu
four complete abandonments	yongs dag spong ba bzhi	
four complete purities	yongs dag bzhi	
four factors of miraculous powers	rdzu 'phrul gyi rkang pa bzhi	
four mindfulnesses	dran pa nyer bzhag bzhi	
four modes of understanding	tshul bzhi	
Four Noble Truths	'phags pa'i bden pa bzhi	
four principles	rigs pa bzhi	yukti-catuṣṭayam
four reliances	ston pa bzhi	
four seals	phyag rgya bzhi	
four types of bliss	dga' ba bzhi	
freedom from cyclic existence	myang 'das	nirvāṇa
fully ordained monk	dge slong	bhikṣu
fully ordained nun	dge slong ma	bhikṣunī
fundamental basis	kun gzhi	ālaya
fundamental/foundational consciousness	kun gzhi rnam shes	ālayavijñāna
fundamental ignorance	ma rig pa	avidyā
fundamental innate mind of clear light	gnyug ma lhan cig skyes pa'i 'od gsal gyi sems	
Gelug	dge lugs	
general meaning	spyi don	
Generation Stage	bsked rim	
Great Perfection (Dzog-chen)	rdzogs chen	
great empty	stong pa chen po	mahāśūnya
great wonderment	sems hal po	
hand gesture, symbolic (See also seal)	phyag rgya	mudrā
heap of light mantra repetition	phung bzlas	
Hearer's Vehicle	nyan thos kyi theg pa	śrāvakayāna
hidden meaning	sbas don	
Highest Yoga Tantra	rnal 'byor bla med kyi rgyud	mahānuttarayoga-tantra

English	*Tibetan*	*Sanskrit*
identity derived from self-production	bdag las skye ba'i ngo bo nyid	
identitylessness	ngo bo nyid med pa	
illusory body	sgyu lus	
imputed phenomena	kun btags	parikalpana
Individual Vehicle	theg dman	hīnayāna
inherent existence/intrinsic existence	rang bzhin gyis grub pa	svabhāvasiddha
initial stage	las dang po pa	
initiation	dbang	abhiṣeka
permission	rjes gnang	anujñā
inner heat	gtum mo	
inner radiance dharmakāya	ka dag nang gsal gyi chos sku	
interpretable, interpretive	drang don	neyārtha
intrinsic characteristics	rang gi mtshan nyid	svalakṣana
intrinsic identity	rang bzhin gyis grub pa'i ngo bo	svarūpa
Kagyu	bka' rgyud	
Path-and-Fruition (Lam-dre)	lam 'bras	
leap-over practice	thod brgal	
literal meaning	yig don	
Madhyamaka-Prāsaṅgika	dbu ma thal 'gyur	madhyamaka-prāsaṅgika
Mādhyamika-Prāsaṅgika	dbu ma thal 'gyur pa	mādhyamika-prāsaṅgika
male lay practitioner	dge bsnyen	upāsaka
mandala	dkyil 'khor	maṇḍala
manifest phenomena	mngon 'gyur	
mantra repetition of commitment	dam tshig gi bzlas pa	
means of attainment	sgrub thabs	sādhana
meditative stabilization of the appearance of all	kun snang gi ting nge 'dzin	
meditative stabilization of suchness	de kho na nyid kyi ting nge 'dzin	
mental body	yid lus	
method factor (of the path)	thabs kyi cha	
method tantra	thabs kyi rgyud	

English	Tibetan	Sanskrit
Middle Way	dbu ma	madhyamaka
Middle Way proponent	dbu ma pa	mādhyamika
Mind Only	sems tsam	cittamātra
mind training (lo-jong)	blo sbyong	
mixings	bsre ba	
Mother Tantra	ma rgyud	
Mūlasarvāstivādin school	gzhi thams bcad yod par smra pa	mūlasarvāstivādin
nature	rang bzhin	svabhāva
Nine Graded Vehicles	theg pa rim pa dgu	
non-conceptuality	mi rtog pa	
Non-Dual Tantra	gnyis med kyi rgyud	
novice monk	dge tshul	śrāmaṇera
novice nun	dge tshul ma	śrāmaṇerikā
Nyingma school	rnying ma	
objective clear light	yul gyi 'od gsal	
one taste	ro gcig	
other-powered	gzhan dbang can	
outer radiance saṃbhogakāya	lhun grub phyi gsal gyi longs sku	
palanquin-like mantra repetition	khyogs kyi bzlas pa	
parinirvāṇa	mya ngan las 'das pa chen po	parinirvāṇa
perfection of wisdom	shes rab kyi pha rol tu phyin pa	prajñāpāramitā
Performance Tantra	spyod rgyud	caryātantra
potential initiation	nus pa'i dbang	
principle of efficacy	bya ba byed pa'i rigs pa	kāryakaraṇayukti
principle of dependence	bltos pa'i rigs pa	apekṣāyukti
principle of reality	chos nyid kyi rigs pa	dharmatāyukti
principle of valid proof	'thad pa'i rigs pa	upapathisāddhanayukti
pristine awareness	rig pa	
profound path	zab mo'i lam	
purity	ka dag	
rainbow body	mja' lus	
resultant tantra	'bras ba'i rgyud	
resultant vajra holder	'bras bu rdo rje 'dzin pa	

English	Tibetan	Sanskrit
Sakya	sa skya	
Sāṃkhya school	grangs can pa	Sāṃkhya
Sautrāntika school	mdo sde pa	
seal (*see also* hand gesture, symbolic)	phyag rgya	mudrā
secret initiation	gsang dbang	
self-identity	bdag; rang gi ngo bo nyid	
selfless	bdag med	
self-sufficient identity	rang skya thub pa'i ngo bo	
seven branches of the path to enlightenment	byang chub yan lag bdun	
six perfections	phar phyin drug	
six parameters	mtha'i drug	
slightly obscure phenomena	cung zad lhog gyur	
Solitary Realizer's Vehicle	rang sang rgyas kyi theg pa	pratyekabuddha-yāna
spontaneity	lhun grub	
subjective clear light	yul can gyi 'od gsal	
suffering; unsatisfactoriness	sdug bsngal ba	duḥkha
supreme king of actions	las rgyal mchog	
supreme king of the mandala	dkyil 'khor rgyal mchog	
sutra	mdo	sūtra
tantra	rgyud	tantra
tantras of austere awareness	dka' thub rig byed kyi theg pa	
Tantric Vehicle	rgyud theg pa	tantrayāna
ten unwholesome actions	mi dge ba bcu	
thoroughly established phenomena	yongs grub	
Three Baskets	sde snod gsum	Tripiṭaka
three higher trainings	lhag pa'i bslab pa gsum	
three isolations	dben pa gsum	
three kāyas of the base	gzhi dus kyi sku gsum	
three meditative stabilizations	ting nge 'dzin gsum	
tranquil (or calm) abiding	zhi gnas	śamatha
transference of consciousness	'pho ba	
true cessation	'gog pa'i bden pa	
Truth Body	chos sku	dharmakāya
turning of the wheel of Dharma	chos 'khor bskor ba	dharmacakra; pravartana

English	Tibetan	Sanskrit
twelve links (in the chain) of dependent origination	rten 'brel yan lag bcu gnyis	
Universal Vehicle	theg pa chen po	mahāyāna
ultimate deity	don dam pa'i lha	
ultimate meaning	mthar thug gi don	
union of bliss and emptiness	bde stong zung 'jug	
union of the two truths	bden gnyis zung 'jug	
vajra repetition	rdor bzlas	
Vajra Vehicle (Vajrayana)	rdo rje theg pa	vajrayāna
vase initiation	bum pa'i dbang	
vast path	rgya che ba'i lam	
vehicle	theg pa	yāna
vehicle of overpowering means	dbang sgyur thabs kyi theg pa	
very empty	shin tu stong pa	atiśūnya
very obscure phenomena	shin tu lhog gyur	
wheel of Dharma clearly elucidating the distinctions	legs par rnam par phye ba'i chos 'khor	
wheel of Dharma pertaining to the absence of intrinsic characteristics	mtshan nyid med pa'i chos 'khor	
wisdom factor of the path	shes rab kyi cha	
wisdom knowledge initiation	shes rab ye shes kyi dbang	
word initiation	tshig dbang	
wrathful mantra repetition	khro bo'i bzlas pa	
Yoga Tantra	rnal 'byor rgyud	yogatantra
yoga of wind	rlung gi rnal 'byor	prāṇayoga
yoga with signs	mtshan bcas kyi rnal 'byor	
yoga without signs	mtshan med kyi rnal 'byor	
Yogācāra	rnal 'byor spyod pa	

BIBLIOGRAPHY

"P" refers to *The Tibetan Tripiṭaka*, Peking Edition, Tibetan Tripiṭaka Research Institute, Tokyo and Kyoto, 1956; and "Toh." to *A Complete Catalogue of the Tibetan Buddhist Canons*, Sendai: Tohoku Imperial University Press, 1934, an index to the Derge edition of the *bKa' 'gyur* and *bsTan 'gyur*.

Tsongkhapa's *Collected Works* used here is that of the Tashi Lhunpo (bKra shis lhun po) edition, reprinted in New Delhi by Ngawang Gelek Demo, 1980.

WORKS CITED OR REFERRED TO BY HIS HOLINESS:

SUTRAS AND TANTRAS

Cakrasaṃvara Tantra
Tantrarājaśrīlaghusaṃvara
rGyud kyi rgyal po dpal bde mchog nyung ngu
P16, Vol. 2

Compendium of Principles Tantra
Sarvatathāgatatattvasaṃgraha
De bzhin gshegs pa thams cad kyi de kho na nyid bsdus pa
Toh. 479

Descent into Laṅkā Sutra
Laṅkāvatārasūtra
Lang kar gshegs pa'i mdo
P775, Vol. 29
English translation by D. T. Suzuki, *The Lankavatara Sutra*, London: Routledge, 1932.

Guhyasamāja Tantra
Guhyasamājanāmamahākalparāja
gSang ba 'dus pa zhes bya ba brtag pa'i rgyal po chen po
P81, Vol. 3

Heart of Wisdom Sutra
Prajñāhṛdaya/Bhagavatīprajñāpāramitāhṛdayasūtra
Shes rab snying po/bCom ldan 'das ma shes rab kyi pha
rol tu phyin pa'i snying po'i mdo
P160, Vol. 6
English translation by E. Conze, *Buddhist Texts Through
the Ages,* Oxford: Cassirer, 1954, pp. 152–3. Also in
Conze, *Perfect Wisdom: The Short Prajñāpāramitā
Texts,* Devon: Buddhist Publishing Group, 1993.

Hevajra Tantra
Hevajratantrarāja
Kye'i rdo rje zhes bya ba rgyud kyi rgyal po
P10, Vol. 1
English translation by D. L. Snellgrove, *The Hevajra Tantra,*
London Oriental Series, Vol. 6. London: Oxford
University Press, 1959. Reprinted 1964, 1971.

Individual Liberation Sutra
Prātimokṣasūtra
So sor thar pa'i mdo
P1031, Vol. 42

Kālacakra Tantra
Śrīkālacakranāmatantrarāja
dPal dus kyi 'khor lo'i rgyud kyi rgyal po
P4, Vol. 1

Nanda's Entry into the Womb
Āyuṣmannandagarbhāvakrāntinirdeśa
Tshe dang ldan pa dga' bo mngal du 'jug pa bstan pa
P760.13, Vol. 23

Perfect Expression of Mañjuśrī's Name Tantra
Āryamañjuśrīnāmasaṃgiti
'Phags pa 'jam dpal gyi msthan yang dag par brjod pa
P2, Vol. 1

Perfection of Wisdom Sutras
Prajñāpāramitāsūtra
Shes rab kyi pha rol tu phyin pa'i mdo
This large category of sutras includes, among others,
    *Eight Thousand Verses on the Perfection of Wisdom, The
    Diamond Cutter Sutra,* and the popular *Heart of
    Wisdom Sutra.*
For English translations, see entry for *Heart of Wisdom
    Sutra* above. Also E. Conze, *The Large Sutra on Perfect
    Wisdom with the divisions of the Abhisamayālankāra,*
    Berkeley: University of California Press, 1975.

Rice Seedling Sutra
Śālistambasūtra
Sā lu'i ljang pa'i mdo
P876, Vol. 34

Sutra Unravelling the Thought of the Buddha
Saṃdhinirmocanasūtra
dGongs pa nges par 'grel pa'i mdo
P774, Vol. 29

Tathāgata Essence Sutra
Tathāgatagarbhasūtra
De bzhin gshegs pa'i snying po'i mdo
P924, Vol. 36; Toh. 258

Vajra-Pinnacle Tantra
Vajraśekharamahāguhyayogatantra
gSang ba rnal' 'byor chen po'i rgyud rdo rje rtse mo
P113, Vol. 5

Vajra-Tent Tantra
Vajrapañjaratantra / Ḍākinīvajrapañjaramahātantra-
rājakalpa
mKa' 'gro ma rdo rje gur zhes bya ba'i rgyud kyi gyal po
chen po'i brtag pa
P11, Vol. 1

Wisdom Vajra Compendium
Jñānavajrasamuccayanāmatantra
Ye shes rdo rje kun las btus pa
P84, Vol. 3

TREATISES AND COMMENTARIAL MATERIAL

Āryadeva
Catuḥśatakaśāstrakārikā
(Four Hundred Verses on the Middle Way)
bsTan bcos bzhi brgya pa zhes bya ba'i tshig le'ur byas pa
P5246, Vol. 95
For English translations see Lang, K. (trans.) *Aryadeva's*
Catuḥśataka: On the Bodhisattva's Cultivation of Merit
and Knowledge. Indiske Studier, Vol. VII. Copen-
hagen: Akademish Forlag, 1986; also by Geshe
Sonam Rinchen, translated by Ruth Sonam, *Yogic*
Deeds of the Bodhisattvas: Gyeltsap on Aryadeva's Four
Hundred, Ithaca: Snow Lion, 1994.

Aśvaghoṣa
Gurupañcāśikā
(Fifty Verses on the Guru)
Bla ma lnga bcu pa
P4544, Vol. 81

Bhāvaviveka
Madhyamakahṛdayakārikā
(*Essence of the Middle Way*)
dBu ma'i snying po
P5255, Vol. 96

Buddhapālita
Buddhapālitamūlamadhyamakavṛtti
(*Buddhapālita's Commentary on the Fundamentals of the Middle Way*)
dBu ma rtsa ba'i 'grel pa buddha pā li ta
P5254, Vol. 95

Buddhaśrījñāna
Mañjuśrīmukhāgama
(*Sacred Words of Mañjushrī*)
'Jam dpal dbyangs kyi zhal lung
Toh. 1853–54

Samantabhadranāmasādhana
(*Means of Attainment Entitled "All Goodness"*)
sGrub thabs kun bzang
Toh. 1855

Candrakīrti
Catuḥśatakaṭīkā
(*Commentary on the Four Hundred Verses*)
bZhi brgya pa'i rgya cher 'grel pa
P5266, Vol. 98

Madhyamakāvatāra
(*Entering into the Middle Way*)
dBu ma la 'jug pa
P5261, Vol. 98; P5262, Vol. 98
A complete English translation of this work exists in *The Emptiness*

of Emptiness by C. W. Huntington, Jr. and Geshe Wangchen.
An English translation of the first five chapters by Jeffrey
Hopkins can be found in *Compassion in Tibetan Buddhism*,
Ithaca: Snow Lion, 1980. Also, English translation of the sixth
chapter by Stephen Batchelor is in Geshe Rabten's *Echoes of
Voidness.*

Mūlamadhyamakavṛttiprasannapadā
(*Clear Words*)
dBu ma rtsa ba'i 'grel pa tshig gsal ba
P5269, Vol. 98
An English translation of selected chapters of this work can be
found in M. Sprung's *Lucid Exposition of the Middle Way.*

Pradīpoddyotananāmaṭīkā
(*Clear Lamp*)
'Grel pa sgron gsal
Toh. 1785

Dharmakīrti
Pramāṇavarttikakārikā
(*Commentary on the Compendium of Valid Cognition*)
Tshad ma rnam 'grel gyi tshig le'ur byas pa
P5709, Vol. 130

Dodrup Jigme Tenpai Nyima (rDo grub 'jigs med bstan pa'i nyi ma)
General Exposition of Guhyagarbha
gSang ba snying po'i spyi don
Collected Works, Vol. *ca* (5)
Dodrup Chen Rinpoche, publ., Gangtok, 1975.

Miscellaneous Works on Great Perfection
rDzogs chen gsung thor bu'i skor
Collected Works, Vol. *ca* (5)
Dodrup Chen Rinpoche, publ., Gangtok, 1975.

Jñānagarbha
Satyadvayavibhāga
(*Analysis of the Two Truths*)
bDen gnyis rnam 'byed
Toh. 3881
English translation found in Eckel, M. D. (trans.)
*Jñānagarbha's Commentary on the Distinction Between
the Two Truths.* Albany: SUNY Press, 1986

Kunkhyen Jigme Lingpa (Kun mkhyen jigs med gling pa)
Treasury of Enlightened Attributes
Yon tan mdzod
Collected Works, Vols. *ka* (1) and *kha* (2)

Longchen Rabjampa (Klong chen rab 'byams pa)
Treasury of the Expanse of Reality
Chos dbyings mdzod
Collected Works, Vol. *kha* (2)

Treasury of the Supreme Vehicle
Theg mchog mdzod
Collected Works, Vols. *ga* (3) and *nga* (4).

Maitreya
Madhyāntavibhāga
(*Discriminating the Middle Way from the Extremes*)
dBus dang mtha' rnam par 'byed pa
P5522, Vol. 108

Mahāyāna-uttaratantraśāstra (*Uttaratantra*)
(*Sublime Continuum of the Great Vehicle*)
Theg pa chen po rgyud bla ma'i bstan bcos
P5525, Vol. 108

P5525, Vol. 108

English translations by E. Obermiller, "Sublime Science of the Great Vehicle to Salvation," in *Acta Orientalia*, 9 (1931), pp. 81–306 and J. Takasaki, *A Study on the Ratnagotravibhāga*, Rome: I.S.M.E.O., 1966; English translation from the Tibetan by Ken and Katia Holmes, *The Changeless Nature*, Dumfriesshire: Karma Drubgyud Darjay Ling, 1985.

Nāgārjuna
Mūlamadhyamakakārikā
    (*Fundamentals of the Middle Way*)
    dBu ma rtsa ba'i tshig le'ur byas pa
    P5224, Vol. 95

English translation by F. Streng, *Emptiness: A Study in Religious Meaning*, Nashville and New York: Abingdon Press, 1967; see also, K. Inada, *Nāgārjuna: A Translation of His Mūlamadhyamakakārikā*, Tokyo: Hokuseido Press, 1970.

Pañcakrama
    (*Five Stages*)
    Rim pa lnga pa
    P2667, Vol. 61

Ratnāvalī
    (*Precious Garland*)
    Rin po che'i 'phreng ba
    P5658, Vol. 129

English translation from the Tibetan by Lati Rinpoche and J. Hopkins as "The Precious Garland of Advice for the King" in the Dalai Lama, et al., *The Buddhism of Tibet*, Ithaca: Snow Lion, 1987 pp. 105–206. See also by G. Tucci (ed. and trans.), "The Ratnāvalī of

Nāgārjuna" in *JRAS*, 1934, pp. 307–25; 1936, pp. 237–52, 423–35.

Śāntideva
Bodhicaryāvatāra
(*Guide to the Bodhisattva's Way of Life*)
Byang chub sems pa'i spyod pa la 'jug pa
P5272, Vol. 99
English translations from the Sanskrit by Marion L. Matics, *Entering the Path of Enlightenment,* New York: Macmillan, 1970, and Parmananda Sharma, *Śāntideva's Bodhicharyāvatāra,* New Delhi: Aditya Prakashan, 1990 (2 volumes); English translation from the Tibetan by Stephen Batchelor, *A Guide to the Bodhisattva's Way of Life,* Dharamsala: Library of Tibetan Works and Archives, 1979.

Tsongkhapa (Tsong kha pa)
Great Exposition of Secret Mantra
sNgags rim chen mo
Collected Works, Vol. *ga* (3).
English Translation of the first two sections by Jeffrey Hopkins in *Tantra in Tibet,* London: George Allen and Unwin, 1977.

Great Exposition of the Stages of the Path
Byang chub lam gyi rim pa chen mo
Collected Works, Vol. *pa* (13).
English translations of the sections on "Concentration" and "Special Insight," by Elizabeth Napper, *Dependent-Arising and Emptiness,* London: Wisdom Publications, 1989 (partial translation), and Alex Wayman, *Calming the Mind and Discerning the Real,* New York: Columbia University Press, 1978.

Vasubandhu
Abhidharmakośakārikā
(*Treasury of Knowledge*)
Chos mngon pa'i mdzod kyi tshig le'ur byas pa
P5590, Vol. 115

Viṃśatikā
(*Twenty Verses*)
Nyi shu pa'i tsig le'ur byas pa
Toh. 4056

WORKS REFERRED TO IN THE TRANSLATOR'S NOTES:

Asaṅga
Abhidharmasamuccaya
(*Compendium of Knowledge*)
mNgon pa kun las bstus pa
P5550, Vol. 112
French translation by Wapola Rahula, *Le Compendium de
la Super-Doctrine (Philosophie D'Asanga)*, Paris: École
Française d'Extrême-Orient, 1971.

Śrāvakabhūmi
(*Levels of Hearers*)
Nyan thos kyi sa
P5537, Vol. 110

Batchelor, S. (trans.) *A Guide to the Bodhisattva's Way of Life.*
Dharamsala: Library of Tibetan Works & Archives, 1979.

Bhāvaviveka
Madhyamakahṛdayavṛtti-tarkajvālā
(*Blaze of Reasoning*)
dBu ma'i snying po'i 'grel pa rtog ge 'bar ba
P5256, Vol. 96

English translation of chapter 3 by S. Iida, *Reason and Emptiness*, Tokyo: Hokuseido, 1980, pp. 52–242.

Butön (Bu ston)
History of Kālacakra
Dus 'khor chos byung
Collected Works, Vol. nga (4).

Chang, Garma C. C. *Teachings of Tibetan Yoga*, New York: University Books, 1963. Reprinted as *The Six Yogas of Naropa*. Ithaca: Snow Lion, 1986.

Changkya Rolpai Dorje (lCang skya rol pa'i rdo rje)
Presentation of Philosophical Systems: The Ornament Beautifying the Buddha's Doctrine
Grub pa'i mtha'i rnam par bzhag pa gsal bar bshad pa thub bstan lhun po'i mdzes rgyan
Sarnath: The Pleasure of Elegant Sayings, 1970.

Conze, E. (trans.) *Buddhist Texts Through the Ages*. Oxford: Cassirer, 1954.

———— (trans.) *The Large Sutra on Perfect Wisdom with the divisions of the Abhisamayālaṅkāra*. Berkeley and Los Angeles: University of California Press, 1975.

———— (trans.) *Perfect Wisdom: The Short Prajñāpāramitā Texts*, Devon: Buddhist Publishing Group, 1993.

———— (trans.) *The Perfection of Wisdom in 8,000 Lines and its Verse Summary*. Bolinas: Four Seasons, 1973.

Cozort, Daniel. *Highest Yoga Tantra*. Ithaca: Snow Lion, 1986.

The Dalai Lama (Fourteenth), Tenzin Gyatso. "Heart of Mantra" in Jeffrey Hopkins (trans.) *The Yoga of Tibet,* London: George Allen and Unwin, 1981 (reprinted as *Deity Yoga,* Ithaca: Snow Lion, 1987), pp. 19-42.

————. *A Flash of Lightning in the Dark of Night.* Boston: Shambhala, Publishing, 1994.

————. *The Meaning of Life from a Buddhist Perspective.* Boston: Wisdom Publications, 1992. Translated and edited by Jeffrey Hopkins.

————. *Path to Bliss: A Practical Guide to the Stages of Meditation.* Ithaca: Snow Lion, 1991. Translated and edited by Geshe Thupten Jinpa; associate editor, Christine Cox.

————. *Transcendent Wisdom.* Ithaca: Snow Lion, 1988. Translated, edited and annotated by B. Alan Wallace.

The Dalai Lama & Jeffrey Hopkins. *Kālachakra Tantra, Rite of Initiation.* Boston: Wisdom, 1985.

The Dalai Lama et al. *The Buddhism of Tibet.* Ithaca: Snow Lion, 1987.

Dudjom Rinpoche. *The Nyingma School of Tibetan Buddhism.* Boston: Wisdom, 1992. Translated and edited by Gyurme Dorje and Matthew Kapstein.

Guenther, H. *Life and Teachings of Naropa.* Oxford: Oxford University Press, 1963.

Holmes, Ken and Katia. *The Changeless Nature.* Dumfriesshire: Karma Drubgyud Darjay Ling, 1985.

Hopkins, J. *Meditation on Emptiness*. Boston: Wisdom, 1983.

———— (transl). *The Yoga of Tibet*. London: George Allen and Unwin, 1981. Reprinted as *Deity Yoga*. Ithaca: Snow Lion, 1987.

Huntington, C. W., Jr. and Geshe Wangchen. *The Emptiness of Emptiness*. Hawaii: University of Hawaii Press, 1989.

Kapstein, M. "Mipham's Theory of Interpretation" in Donald Lopez (ed.) *Buddhist Hermeneutics* (Delhi: Motilal Banarsidass, 1993), pp. 149–74.

Geshe Kelsang Gyatso. *Clear Light of Bliss*. 1982. London: Tharpa, 1992. Translated by Tenzin Norbu; edited by Jonathan Landaw.

Kongtrul Yönten Gyatso (Kong sprul yon tan rgya mtsho)
Treasury of Encyclopedic Knowledge
Shes bya kun khyab mdzod
Beijing: Minorities Press, 1983.

Lati Rinpoche, Denma Lochoe Rinpoche, L. Zahler & J. Hopkins. *Meditative States in Tibetan Buddhism*. Boston: Wisdom Publications, 1983.

Lati Rinpoche & Jeffrey Hopkins *Death, Intermediate State and Rebirth in Tibetan Buddhism*, London: Rider and Company, 1979.

————. "The Precious Garland of Advice for the King" in the Dalai Lama, et al. *The Buddhism of Tibet*. 1975. Ithaca: Snow Lion Publications, 1987, pp. 105–206.

Lopez, Jr., Donald (ed.) *Buddhist Hermeneutics*. Delhi: Motilal Banarsidass, 1993.

Matics, Marion L. (trans.) *Entering the Path of Enlightenment*. New York: Macmillan, 1970.

Ngawang Palden (Ngag dbang dpal ldan)
Presentation of the Grounds and Paths of the Four Great Secret Tantra Classes
gSang chen rgyud sde bzhi'i sa lam gyi rnam gzhag
Collected Works, Vol. *kha* (2).

Obermiller, E. "Sublime Science of the Great Vehicle to Salvation" in *Acta Orientalia*, 9 (1931), pp. 81–306.

Pabongka Rinpoche. *Liberation in the Palm of Your Hand*. Edited by Trijang Rinpoche; translated by Michael Richards. Boston: Wisdom Publications, 1992.

Kulika Puṇḍarīka.
Vimalaprabhā
(Stainless Light)
'Grel chen dri med 'od
P2064, Vol. 46

Geshe Rabten. *Echoes of Voidness*. Translated by Stephen Batchelor. Boston: Wisdom Publications, 1983.

Roerich, G. (trans.). *The Blue Annals*. Delhi: Motilal Benarsidass, 1979. An English translation of Gö Lotsawa Shönu Pal's *Deb ther sngon po*.

Sharma, Parmananda. *Śāntideva's Bodhicharyāvatāra*. New Delhi: Aditya Prakashan, 1990 (2 volumes).

Shastri, D. (ed.). *Tattvasaṃgraha*. Varanasi: Bauddha Bharati, 1968.

Sprung, M. *Lucid Exposition of the Middle Way*. Boulder: Prajna, 1979.

Streng, F. *Emptiness: A Study in Religious Meaning.* Nashville and New York: Abingdon, 1967.

Suzuki, D.T. *The Lankavatara Sutra.* London: Routledge and Kegan Paul, 1956.

Takasaki, J. *A Study on the Ratnagotravibhāga.* Rome: I.S.M.E.O., 1966.

Thuken Chökyi Nyima (Thu'u bkwan chos kyi nyi ma)
Crystal Mirror of Philosophical Systems
Grub mtha' shal gyi me long
Collected Works, Vol. 2, Kansu: Minorities Press, 1984 (typeset edition).

Thurman, R. *The Central Philosophy of Tibet: A Study and Translation of Jey Tsong Khapa's Essence of True Eloquence.* Princeton: Princeton University Press, 1984.

———. "Vajra Hermeneutics" in Donald Lopez, Jr. (ed.) *Buddhist Hermeneutics,* Delhi: Motilal Banarsidass, 1993, pp. 119–48.

Tsongkhapa (Tsong kha pa).
Commentary on the Profound Path of the Six Yogas of Naropa Endowed with Three Convictions
Zab lam naro chos drug gi krid yid ched gsum ldan
Collected Works, Vol. *ta* (9)

Essence of True Eloquence: Treatise Discriminating the Interpretable and the Definitive
Drang ba dang nges pa'i don rnam par phye ba'i bstan bcos legs bshad snying po
Collected Works, Vol. *pha* (13)
English translation by R. Thurman, *The Central Philosophy of Tibet,* Princeton: Princeton University Press, 1984.

Exposition of the Wisdom Vajra Compendium
dPal gsang ba 'dus pa'i bshad pa'i rgyud ye shes rdo rje kun las
btus pa'i rgya cher bshad pa / rGyud bshad thabs kyi man ngag
gsal bar bstan pa
Collected Works, Vol. *ca* (5)

*Golden Rosary of Eloquence: An Extensive Exposition of the
Abhisamayālaṃkāra and its Commentary*
Legs bshad gser gyi phreng ba/Sherab kyi pha rol tu phyin pa'i
man ngag gi bstan bcos mngon par rtog pa'i rgyan 'grel pa
dang bcas pa'i rgya cher bshad pa
Collected Works, Vols. *tsa* (17) and *tsha* (18)

Lamp Brilliantly Illuminating the Five Stages
Rim pa lnga rab tu gsal ba'i sgron me
Collected Works, Vol. *ja* (7).

Tucci, Giuseppe, (ed. and trans.). "The Ratnāvalī of Nāgārjuna" in
JRAS, 1934, pp. 307–25; 1936, pp. 237–52, 423–35.

Williams, P. *Mahayana Buddhism*. New York: Routledge, 1989.

INDEX

distractions, avoiding 94–95, 138, 151
divine pride. *See* identity as a deity
Dodrup Jigme Tenpai Nyima (*rDo
grub 'jigs med bstan pa'i nyi ma*)
119–120, 129, 149, 173
Dorje, Gyurme 170
dream state 96, 142–143
dualistic appearances 98
Dudjom Rinpoche 147, 167, 170
duḥkha (Skt.) 38, 159. *See also*
suffering/unsatisfactoriness
Dzog-chen 104, 119, **129**, 143,
145–146, 149–150, 166. *See also*
Great Perfection; breakthrough;
leap-over
three faculties seen in 149–150
E-VAM 131
eating meat 112
eightfold noble path 21
Emanation Body (Skt. *nirmāṇakāya*)
135, 138, 169
emotional and cognitive
experiences 32
states (afflictive) 10, 20, 97, 100
empowerment. *See* initiation/
empowerment
emptiness **25**
and dependent origination 34, 42,
45–46
as creator of samsara and nirvana 120
experience of 23–24, 30, 97,
133–134
four phases of (in Guhyasamāja) 148
interpretations of 28–29, 35,
43–44, 54, 145, 148–149
meditation on. *See* meditation on
emptiness
objective 101, 149
of other. *See* Shen-tong
pure. *See* pure emptiness
realization of/understanding of 11,
24, 26–27, 32–33, 54, 75, 97,
99, 101, 123, 133–134, 142,
148–150, 170

subjective 27, 101, 149
ultimate view of 31, 42–44, 162
view of 28, 43, 55, 93, 133, 144,
146, 159
"empty" 148
empty form 143, 172
empty nature
of phenomena 42, 44–45, 87
of the deity 99, 116–119
of the mind 101
enemies
internal and external 67–73, 75
kindness of 81–82
energy winds. *See* winds
Enjoyment Body. *See* Complete
Enjoyment Body
enlightened being. *See* buddha;
bodies of an enlightened being
enlightened body/speech/mind 115,
120
enlightenment **11**–13, 15, 27, 42,
100, 113, 143, 158, 165. *See also*
buddhahood
mind of 80, 85, 89, 94, 97, 101,
167
path to 11, 13, 16, 20–21, 24,
26–27, 65, 93–94, 97
equalizing and exchanging 85
essence of buddhahood **27**, 94. *See
also* buddha-nature
Essence of True Eloquence (*Legs bshad
snying po*) 160–161
ethics
training in 18–20, 65, 108, 158
expanse of reality 32, 120
explicit and implicit. *See also*
interpretation of scripture
levels of meaning 129–130
readings 26, 30
Father Tantra 104–**105**
first turning 15, 17–25, 27, 31, 158
five clarifications 138, **171**
five faculties 21
five powers 21

threefold division 105
Hinayana 10, 31, 33, 113. *See also*
Theravāda; lower schools
History of Kālacakra (*Dus 'khor chos
byung*) 165
Holmes, Ken and Katia 161
Hopkins, Jeffrey 159–160, 164–165,
167–169
Huntington, Jr., C. W. 161–162
identity as a deity **100**, 118, 138,
169. *See also* deity yoga
identity derived from self-production
28
identitylessness 28
ignorance **38**
antidote to 17, 20
fundamental 10–11, **17**, 38, 74
illusory body **127**, 130, 132, 143,
148, 171–172
imagination 97, 116–119, 121,
136–137
impermanence 31, **37**–38, 159
imputation 50–**52**, 133
imputed phenomena. *See* phenomena,
imputed
Individual Liberation Sutra (*Prātimokṣasūtra*) 19
inherent existence 23, 27–29, 33,
35, 50, **52**, 54, 116, 145
initiation/empowerment **105–109**,
111, 132, 150, 154, 171
innate mind of clear light. *See* clear
light, innate mind of
inner heat 133–134, 172. *See also*
tantra, physiological aspects
inner radiance dharmakāya 144
inner strength 64, 82
inner tantras/inner vehicles 104
inner world 72
insight 17, 20, **24**, 71–72, 75, 142.
See also wisdom
special 121–123
interdependence 34. *See also*
dependent origination

interpretable scriptures 25, 41–43
interpretation of scripture 25, 30,
41–43, 129–131, 147, 170. *See
also* explicit and implicit
intrinsic identity
ascribed to phenomena 28, 32
denial of 28, 33
isolations. *See* three isolations
je-nang (Tib.). *See* permission
jin-lab (Tib.). *See* blessing
Jñānapāda school 166
Jonangpa school 162
Kagyu 128, 143
Kālacakra (wheel of time) 142, 165,
167
Kālacakra Tantra 48, 96, 108, 127,
142–143, 148, 160, 165,
167–168, 172
Kangyur 160
Kapstein, Matthew 163
karma. See cause and effect;
conditioned existence
Kelsang Gyatso (Geshe) 172
Khedup Norsang Gyatso (*mKhas
grub nor bzang rgya mtsho*) 166
kindness 3, 63, 65, 82
of the enemy 81
Kongtrul Yönten Gyatso (*Kong sprul
yon tan rgya mtsho*) 168
Kunkhyen Jigme Lingpa (*Kun
mkhyen jigs med gling pa*) 145
Kunu Lama Rinpoche (*bsTan 'dzin
rgyal mtshan*) 59, 75
Lam-dre 119, 143
lama. *See* guru
*Lamp Brilliantly Illuminating the Five
Stages* (*Rim pa lnga rab tu gsal ba'i
sgron me*) 166, 170
Lati Rinpoche 157, 159, 164, 169
lay practitioner 113, 141
leap-over practice 144. *See also*
Dzog-chen
literal meaning 25, 44, **130–131**
lo-jong (Tib.). *See* mind training

WISDOM PUBLICATIONS

Wisdom publications is a non-profit publisher of books on Buddhism, Tibet, and related East-West themes. Our titles are published in appreciation of Buddhism as a living philosophy and with the special commitment to preserve and transmit important works from all the major Buddhist traditions.

If you would like more information, a copy of our extensive mail order catalogue, or to be kept informed about our future publications, please write or call us at 361 Newbury Street, Boston, Massachusetts, 02115. Telephone: (617) 536-3358. Fax: (617) 536-1897

THE WISDOM TRUST

As a non-profit publisher, Wisdom is dedicated to the publication of fine Dharma books for the benefit of all sentient beings. We depend upon sponsors in order to publish books like the one you are holding in your hand.

If you would like to make a donation to the Wisdom Trust Fund to help us continue our Dharma work or to receive information about opportunities for planned giving, please write to our Boston office.

Thank you so much.

Wisdom is a non-profit, charitable 501(c)(3) organization and a part of the Foundation for the Preservation of the Mahayana Tradition (FPMT).

Care of Dharma Books

DHARMA BOOKS contain the teachings of the Buddha; they have the power to protect against lower rebirth and to point the way to liberation. Therefore, they should be treated with respect—kept off the floor and places where people sit or walk—and not stepped over. They should be covered or protected for transporting and kept in a high, clean place separate from more "mundane" materials. Other objects should not be placed on top of Dharma books and materials. Licking the fingers to turn pages is considered bad form (and negative karma). If it is necessary to dispose of Dharma materials, they should be burned rather than thrown in the trash. When burning Dharma texts, it is considered skillful to first recite a prayer or mantra, such as OM, AH, HUNG. Then, you can visualize the letters of the texts (to be burned) absorbing into the AH, and the AH absorbing into you. After that, you can burn the texts.

These considerations may also be kept in mind for Dharma artwork, as well as the written teachings and artwork of other religions.

Wisdom Publications